Celebrate Christmas

Christmas Sketches & Plays for Your Church

Volume 1

randall house
www.RandallHouse.com

Celebrate Christmas
Published by Randall House Publications
114 Bush Road / PO Box 17306
Nashville, Tennessee 37217

© Copyright 2007
Randall House Publications

Additional copies of this book may be purchased at
www.RandallHouse.com or by calling 1-800-877-7030.

Printed in the United States of America

10-digit ISBN 0892655860
13-digit ISBN 9780892655861

Table of Contents

Alice and the Christmas Ride

by Suzanne Hadley

Characters: -Alice
-Alice's thoughts (pre-recorded, or voiced by another actor)
-Voice (off stage)
-Homeless people (1-3)
-Extras (1-3)
-Mary
-Joseph

Purpose: To communicate the truth that Jesus offered salvation to every person when He humbled Himself to be born in a stable. This skit will encourage viewers to take their eyes off their own busyness this season and focus on opportunities to offer Christ's love to those in need.

Production: Scene 1 is a table of sweaters for sale in a department store. Scene 2 is a street scene outside the store. End the production with a live nativity scene.

Props: Table, several folded sweaters, sign on table that reads, "Sweaters—half price," backdrop of inside of store, backdrop of a street scene, a few blankets, prerecorded Christmas music, costumes for Mary and Joseph, a manger

Length: 10 minutes

Scene 1:

Inside a department store. Christmas music is playing loudly. Alice crosses stage with full shopping bags and stops in front of a table of sweaters.

Alice's thoughts: *(Browsing items)* OK, focus. I still need to get something for Janet. *(Looks at list)* Oh! And the girls at the office. The sooner I get out of here the better. If I hear "Jingle Bells" one more time . . .

Alice: Why do I put myself through this?

Alice's thoughts: I should just give them all gift certificates and get it over with.

Alice: *(Sighs)* Mom would be disappointed.

Alice's thoughts: Oh well, it's just one more thing on the list of holiday woe. The office Christmas party: "No date, Alice?"

Alice: *(Gasp)* Shocker!

Alice's thoughts: And, of course, the writing of my yearly Christmas letter where I have to sound moderately successful and happy with my life: "This year I've particularly enjoyed knitting and spending time with my cat." And now the endless task of picking out just the right cheap, meaningless trinkets for my coworkers and a sweater my sister will actually wear. *(Holds up a sweater. Puts it back.)* When did I turn into Scrooge? I used to like the holidays. I know Jesus-is-the-Reason-for-the-Season and all that, but I'm too stressed out to care. It's like an amusement park ride. I got on, and now I can't get off. *(Music goes down.)*

Voice: Your attitude should be the same as that of Christ Jesus. *(Music goes up.)*

Alice: Ugh! What is with this music? *(Turns for one last look at the store before exiting)*

Alice's thoughts: Why can't I get off the ride?

Scene 2:

Outside on the street. City sounds. Alice comes on stage carrying shopping bags, in a hurry.

Homeless man: Can you spare some change, Miss?

Alice:	Uh, sorry, I don't have any. *(Hurries past)*
Alice's thoughts:	I feel bad for him, but there's not really anything I can do. Besides, I can guess what he'd spend it on. *(Noise goes down.)*
Voice:	Your attitude should be the same as that of Christ Jesus.

(An Extra enters handing out blankets to homeless. Alice, about to exit stage, turns around and observes.)

Alice's thoughts:	I'm glad someone's helping. It must be hard to be homeless at Christmas. Those people are so grateful for those blankets . . .
Alice:	And peanut butter and jelly sandwiches!
Alice's thoughts:	I never have to worry where my next meal will come from, and I'm still not happy. What is Christmas like on the street? Not about gifts and parties and looking like you have it all together . . . *(Sits down on edge of stage. Pulls out a tissue-wrapped package from her bag. She unwraps it and pulls out nativity scene manger with baby Jesus.)*
Alice:	You knew what it was like to be homeless at Christmas.
Alice's thoughts:	Born to a poor carpenter . . . in a barn.
Voice:	"Being in very nature God, He did not consider equality with God something to be grasped, but made himself nothing."
Alice's thoughts:	Your family didn't have the best reputation either.
Voice:	"Taking the very nature of a servant."
Alice:	Why would God come to earth like that?
Voice:	"Being made in human likeness."
Alice's thoughts:	He could have come in any other way.
Voice:	"And being found in appearance as a man."
Alice's thoughts:	He was all-powerful God.
Voice:	"He humbled himself."
Alice:	Why did He choose to be poor?

Voice: "And became obedient to death—even death on a cross."
(Play "Away in a Manger" or another song about the manger. As song begins, Alice is still reflecting on the small manger scene. Create a live nativity on the opposite side of the stage. Alice's attention turns to the live nativity as the homeless approach the manger.)

Alice's thoughts: I guess Jesus humbled Himself so no one would be left out. No one would see salvation as out of reach. God made Himself nothing, so those who have nothing could know Him.

Alice: Do I have that kind of humility?

Voice: Your attitude should be the same as that of Christ Jesus.

Alice's thoughts: Or am I too caught up in my own, comfortable life?

Voice: Your attitude should be the same as that of Christ Jesus.

Alice's thoughts: What does that humility look like? The kind that says, "I will make myself small and poor so you can know me . . . and through me, know Him."

Voice: Your attitude should be the same as that of Christ Jesus.

Alice's thoughts: Maybe it's seeking out those people who need Him most—the hurting and lonely. Or sacrificing something I'm holding on to.

Alice: Maybe it's just stopping the ride and getting off.

(Alice stands. Leaving her bags behind, she crosses stage and kneels by the manger scene. Others may come from congregation and kneel by the manger.)

Thou Didst Leave Thy Throne

by Kenneth Carr

Characters: -Readers (You may use as many readers as you like)
-Choir (Choir can consist of various age groups and size. Soloist can even be used for these parts)

Purpose: "Thou Didst Leave Thy Throne" was written to emphasize the scriptural truths of the words of the hymn. Thoughtful worship and active participation in this production will hopefully render deep response to the gospel.

Production: Set the stage for readers and choir participation. Be sure microphones are readily available and properly placed.

Props: None necessary

Length: 8-10 minutes

Reader: "Ye know the grace of our Lord Jesus Christ, that, though he was rich, yet for your sakes he became poor, that ye, through his poverty might be rich." *(2 Corinthians 8:9)*

(Note: The Scripture reference is given for reference only if the Reader wishes to use another translation. Scripture reference is not meant to be read aloud by Reader. All reference printed in "Thou Didst Leave Thy Throne" are from the King James Version of the Bible.)

Choir: Thou didst leave Thy throne and Thy kingly crown
When Thou camest to earth for me;
But in Bethlehem's home there was found no room
For Thy holy nativity.
O come to my heart, Lord Jesus:
There is room in my heart for Thee!
(Hymn–"Thou Didst Leave Thy Throne," vs. 1)

Reader: "When the fullness of the time was come, God sent forth his Son, made of a woman, made under the law, To redeem them that were under the law, that we might receive the adoption of sons." *(Galatians 4:4, 5)*

Choir: Heaven's arches rang when the angels sang,
Proclaiming Thy royal degree
But in lowly birth didst Thou come to earth
And in great humility.
O come to my heart, Lord Jesus:
There is room in my heart for Thee! (v. 2)

Reader: "It came to pass, that, as they went in the way, a certain man said unto him, Lord, I will follow thee whithersoever thou goest. And Jesus said unto him, Foxes have holes, and birds of the air have nests; but the Son of man hath not where to lay his head." *(Luke 9:57-58)*

Choir: The foxes found rest, and the birds their nest
In the shade of the forest tree,
But Thy couch was the sod, O Thou Son of God,
In the deserts of Galilee.
O come to my heart, Lord Jesus:
There is room in my heart for Thee! (v.3)

Reader: "The next day John seeth Jesus coming unto him, and saith, Behold the Lamb of God, which taketh away the sin of the world." *(John 1:29)* "And they clothed him with purple, and platted a crown of thorns, and put it about his head, And began to salute him, Hail, King of the Jews! And they smote him on the head with a reed, and did spit upon him, and bowing their knees worshipped him. And when they had mocked him, they took off the purple from him, and put his own clothes on him, and led him out to crucify him." *(Mark 15:17-20)*

Choir:　Thou camest, O Lord, with the living word
　　　　　That should set Thy people free,
　　　　　But with mocking scorn and with crown of thorn
　　　　　They bore Thee to Calvary.
　　　　　O come to my heart, Lord Jesus:
　　　　　There is room in my heart for Thee! (v. 4)

Reader:　"When the Son of man shall come in his glory, and all the holy angels with him, then shall he sit upon the throne of his glory." *(Matthew 25:31)* "Watch therefore: for ye know not what hour your Lord doth come." *(Matthew 24:42)* "If I go and prepare a place for you, I will come again, and receive you unto myself; that where I am, there ye may be also." *(John 14:3)*

Choir:　When the heavens shall ring and the angels sing
　　　　　At Thy coming to victory,
　　　　　Let Thy voice call me home, saying, "Yet there is room,
　　　　　There is room at my side for thee."
　　　　　And my heart shall rejoice, Lord Jesus,
　　　　　When Thou comest and callest me (v. 5)

Beyond the Wood

by Blair L. Martin

Characters: -Ken Roberts, an alpha-type CEO
-Margaret Taylor, Ken's secretary
-Alisha Roberts, Ken's wife

Purpose: In our ever-increasing commercialized world, Christmas has become a mere commodity—a time to spend money—rather than a reflection of a life-changing event. This drama was written with the idea that not only do we place high value on products, but we also devalue the human connections in our lives. Christmas reminds us that Jesus came as an infant to communicate with us—to show us His love—but it wasn't until He died on the cross that we have the full picture.

Production: The two settings (office and home) should be placed on opposite sides of the stage. The home should have a table set for two, as well as a recliner or rocking chair and a stand beside it with magazines and a newspaper. The office can be merely a desk with a typical office look to it. Ken should be played as a cold, matter-of-fact business type. Ironically, Alisha is in better touch with what is good and true and shows a much better understanding of Christmas.

For more dramas from this author visit www.ihgproductions.com

Props: Office desk, chair, accessories (papers, pencils, stapler, phone, etc.), laptop, briefcase, FedEx or UPS express envelope, small wooden Christmas ornament, table, two chairs, dinner setting for two, extra chair, and stand

Length: 6—8 minutes

Scene 1:

Stage Right: The afternoon of Christmas Eve. Ken is finishing a project that must be in the mail on the 26th. Margaret has agreed to stay late and they are the last two in the building.

Ken: *(Into the speaker phone)* Margaret, could you come in for a moment, please? *(After a few moments, Margaret enters carrying some letters, magazines, and a FedEx or UPS express envelope)* Margaret, I appreciate your staying late tonight. How are those charts coming along?

Margaret: As a matter of fact, I was just getting ready to bring them in. *(Hands him a stack of papers; he quickly flips through them)*

Ken: Excellent, Margaret. They'll need to be mailed to the Anderson Group first thing on the 26th.

Margaret: I'll be sure they get in the mail. And here is today's mail. *(Hands him a stack of mail including the package)* If that's everything, I'm going to head home.

Ken: Absolutely, and have a nice Christmas day. *(Margaret turns to leave. Ken holds up the package)* . . . Oh no . . .

Margaret: *(She turns back to the desk)* Bad news?

Ken: You could say that. *(Holding the special delivery envelope)* From my brother.

Margaret: Georgia, right?

Ken: *(With a sarcastic Southern accent)* Yup, in the hills of North Georgia.

Margaret: *(Mimicking the accent)* As in *Deliverance*, "Dueling Banjos"?

Ken: Don't remind me. You know, Ted had the opportunity to go to college but he never did.

Margaret: I thought he owned his own business.

Ken: A garage, for heaven's sake. *(Shaking his head)* And that wife of his—she has this horrendous accent so of course their kids do too. Can you imagine how I dread those lunches where everyone begins to talk about family? *(Pauses thoughtfully)* Don't get me wrong; he has a good heart. You remember what happened last year?

Margaret: You mean your father?

Ken: Yes. *(Pause)* Ted was right there at the end, holding his hand. He made all the arrangements. All I had to do was go down for the funeral. *(Looks at the envelope)* Still though, I wish he would try to better himself. *(Opens the envelop—out comes a small wooden Christmas ornament. Ken sighs in dismay)* See, this is exactly what I'm talking about. I sent him a DVD player and all he can send me is a lousy ornament. And not even a very good-looking one at that.

Margaret: *(Laughingly)* Well, just be thankful that they're not spending Christmas with you.

Ken: *(Also laughs)* Yes, thank goodness for small favors. Well, Margaret. I'll see you in two days.

Margaret: Merry Christmas, Mr. Roberts. Good night. *(She exits)*

Ken closes down computer and begins straightening his desk. He places the charts Margaret brought to one side and begins to toss extra items into the wastebasket. He picks up the ornament, looks at it a moment, and then throws it away. He dumps some other papers on top of it and then exits.

Scene 2:

Stage Left: Mrs. Roberts is putting the finishing touches on the dinner table. She is waiting for Ken to come home. When he walks in the door, she is obviously excited to see him as if she has been hiding something.

Ken: Hi, honey. *(Kisses her lightly, quickly looks at the table and then heads for the end table)* Did we get the *Wall Street Journal* today?

Alisha: We're about ready to sit down and eat. Would you like to tell me about your day? Did anything interesting happen?

Ken: *(Looking for the paper)* Um, no, not really. We finished the Anderson portfolio—should be ready to roll first thing when I get back.

Alisha: *(Fishing for details)* Did you get any special gifts today?

Ken: Just some of the typical office things—you know those people.

Alisha: Nothing in the mail?

Ken: *(Getting irritated)* Alisha, what's this about?

Alisha: I was just wondering . . .

Ken: I *did* get something from Ted today. Is that what you're getting at? Do you know something about it?

Alisha: What did he send you?

Ken: Nothing really. *(Alisha stiffens)* You know what Ted is like. I never expect anything from him anyway.

Alisha: *(Standing still)* Nothing . . .

Ken: Alisha, what's this about?

Alisha: *(Sarcastically)* Where is the "nothing" Ted sent you?

Ken: *(Defensively)* What difference does it make? It was a stupid tree ornament. He probably didn't spend any more than five dollars on it!

Alisha: *(Coldly but with force)* Did you look at it?

Ken: It didn't take long to see it was junk; that's why I tossed it out with the rest of the trash. *(Reaches for her)* Why are you suddenly so . . .

Alisha: Don't touch me.

Ken: Alisha.

Alisha: *(Very deliberately)* If you had cared enough and had taken the time to look at it, you might have seen the initials PR carved onto the bottom of it.

Ken: *(Suddenly quiet)* What are you saying? PR—as in Paul Roberts?

Alisha: Yes, Ken. That was the last thing your father made before he died. He gave it to Ted to give to you. Ted called me last month and told me what he wanted to do. He said he couldn't have asked for a better brother. I'm sorry he was so wrong.

Ken: *(Very defensively)* How was I supposed to know? He should have sent a card with it, or a letter—or you could have given me some warning.

Alisha: *(Sadly)* You're looking anywhere you can to place the blame. *(Pauses, then forcefully)* It's too bad you didn't look beyond the wood and see the love.

MANGER 101

by Kathy Ide (with David B. Carl)

Characters: -Mom, a modern-day, middle-aged mother
-Dad, Mom's husband
-Roy, Mom and Dad's son, late elementary through high school
-Karen, Mom and Dad's daughter, late elementary through high school

Purpose: It's easy to become trapped in the trappings of the holidays, to focus so much on our traditions that we lose sight of the basic message of Christmas. We may set up a beautiful nativity scene, with cows, sheep, clean hay, and a manger . . . but in all our fuss over the details, have we forgotten the baby Jesus? This sketch reminds us that appearances aren't as important as the miraculous appearance of God's Son on this earth.

Production: On the edges of a strip mall parking lot, Christmastime, late afternoon.

Props: No props are necessary, but you could have a manger scene, simple or elaborate. Chairs may also be used. Characters should wear outdoor winter clothing, preferably something "Christmassy."

Length: 15 minutes

Scene 1:

Mom, Dad, Roy, and Karen stand in the parking lot, admiring a (real or imagined) manger scene.

Dad: This manger scene is gonna look great when all the parking lot lights come on.

Roy: It's starting to get dark already.

Karen: Okay, I admit this is kinda cool. Millions of people are going to see the results of my artistic genius.

Dad: Maybe thousands.

Mom: Last year they put us behind the mini-mart. This year everyone going to the mall will see our display.

Karen: This is really putting me into the Christmas spirit. Let's go get a pizza.

Roy: Surprise! She wants to eat again.

Dad: Actually, I am kinda hungry. But I'm thinking something a little more Christ-massy.

Karen: Like what?

Dad: Chinese!

Mom: Figgie pudding and kung pao chicken—the traditional Yuletide feast.

Roy: *(Peering at the manger scene)* Where's the baby?

Mom: The what?

Roy: Well, manger scenes always have a cow, a sheep, some clean hay, and . . .

Mom: *(Suddenly panicked, rummages around the manger scene.)* Where's the baby Jesus?

Karen: *(With some guilt)* The baby who?

Roy: What did you do to baby Jesus?

Dad: Leave your sister alone, Roy.

Mom: I saw it in the trunk just before we left the house.

Roy: Karen did something to the baby Jesus. I just know it!

Karen: Nothing! I did nothing!

Dad: Roy, your sister did not do anything to the baby Jesus.

Karen: I only . . .

Dad: What did you do?

Mom: *(Still rummaging)* I am positive he was in the trunk.

Karen: Oh, he was in the trunk. I just picked him up to look at him. Then I put him in the big box next to the car.

Dad: That's the box I put back in the garage!

Roy: She put the baby Jesus in a trash box! I told you she did something. No one listens to me. Now we have to go home and get him.

Mom: We don't have time. It will be dark in fifteen minutes, tops. As soon as the lights come on, people will start coming by. It will take over an hour to go home and come back.

Dad: What are you suggesting?

Roy: *(Shocked)* We're gonna have a manger scene without a baby Jesus?

Karen: You can't do that. There are . . . rules for . . . mangers. You gotta have a baby Jesus.

Mom: It'll just be for tonight. Tomorrow I'll come back and put him in the hay where he belongs.

Karen: That'll work.

Dad: *(Shaking his head)* I married Scrooge.

Mom: No one will notice. *(Adjusting the scene)* I'll just tilt the manger away from the lights. You can't see it from the street anyway.

Dad: After that, we can set the Christmas tree on fire and beat up some cute elves.

Roy: Come on, Mom. You gotta have a baby Jesus. That's the whole point.

Karen: I hate to admit it, but I think Roy's right.

Mom: Let's be practical here. We can either have a manger where people *know* the baby Jesus is missing, or we'll have a manger that has no baby Jesus, but people will *think* it does. *(Pause)* I vote for "think it does." *(They all look at one another, considering the options.)*

Mom: That, or one of you kids could curl up in a tiny ball and pretend to be the baby Jesus.

Roy: No way.

Karen: I vote for "think it does."

Dad: I don't know.

Mom: Come on, honey. You see a nice manger scene and you just assume Jesus is in there. It's pretty, it makes you feel good, and you go on your way. You don't go poking around looking for him. It just isn't done.

Dad: *(Shrugs)* Makes sense to me.

Karen: So does this mean we can go get Chinese food now?

Mom: I'm ready!

They all exit, talking excitedly about what they plan to order. Roy, exiting last, turns for one final look at the manger scene. After a brief expression of concern, he shrugs and joins the others.

Roy: Hey, you guys, wait for me!

The True Meaning of Christmas

by David Amburgey

Characters: -Two ladies
-Salesperson
-Store customers
-Unnamed man

Purpose: "The True Meaning of Christmas" shows how we as a society have taken the most extraordinary time of the year and made it mundane. Each year at Christmas we are all excited about the magic of the surrounding time, but are soon lost in the commercialism that surround us. With this we seem to lose the true meaning of Christmas.

Production: The stage is set up like the toy department of a department store full of busy Christmas shoppers. On one side of the stage, set up a Customer Service counter.

Props: Items to turn the stage into the toy department of a department store (this can be done by painting backdrops or using tables and shelves to mimic displayed merchandise), a toy robot display, identical boxes containing imaginary Zurphie robots (again the robot display can be a painted backdrop), signs, phone

Length: 12-15 minutes

Scene 1:

Two ladies enter the stage talking to each other. They are inside a store Christmas shopping. There are several others in the background milling around, shopping. The stage is set up like a department store and is filled with customers.

First lady: *(She comes to an item sitting on display in the store and her eyes light up. She is giddy with excitement)* Here it is. *(She picks up the item and studies it carefully, smiling)* Yes, that is exactly what Zack wants. He is about to go crazy for one of these things and I'm afraid if he doesn't get it, it will ruin Christmas. *(She sighs deeply)* He doesn't want anything else.

Second lady: Well, you'd better get it; it's the last one. *(She pauses to read the sign that was below the item)* Oh, no, wait a minute. The sign says, "Display item only." *(She looks around)* They must be handing them out somewhere else. And look, this one has a wire attached to the bottom of it. *(She shakes her head in disbelief)* I guess they can't trust anybody these days. The way some people act at Christmas is horrible.

First lady: I know! This is the time for peace and love. People can't even be trusted with a little toy anymore. Everything is so commercial these days.

Second lady: *(Shaking her head again)* Yeah, I know, it's terrible. People just get caught up in a mad rush to buy things and forget about the true meaning of Christmas. *(She pauses. The two ladies are walking again)* What is so special about the Zurphie Robot anyway?

First lady: Oh, it's pretty amazing. It walks and talks; it can teach kids math, reading, and spelling—and it can learn! It can become a kid's best friend. *(She looks at her and changes her voice a bit as if she is telling a great secret)* Honey, this thing would be a great babysitter while I take a hot bath.

Second lady: Boys are so complicated to shop for. With my daughters all I have to do is get them one of those MP3 players, a couple of CDs, clothes, perfume, and jewelry, and they're happy.

First lady: *(Shakes her head in agreement as her attention begins to be drawn away to the surrounding atmosphere)* I just love Christmas . . . all the lights and decorations. The music. The shopping. Everything about Christmas just makes me feel like a kid again. *(She is smiling and looking up at the music as if she could see the beauty in the words)*

Second lady: Oh, look. There's a line. I wonder if that is the line for the Zurphies?

First lady: Let's go find out.

The lights dim as the ladies exit.

Scene 2:

A salesperson is standing behind the counter. He looks tired and frustrated. Behind him is a stack of Zurphie Robots still in the box. Above him is a sign that says, "Limit, 2 per customer."

Salesperson:	*(He is craning to one side looking at the long line. The two ladies from Scene 1 are about two-thirds of the way back in that line. He sighs and returns to the normal standing position and blankly stares at the next person in line.)* One or two? *(His voice is monotone and obviously unexcited)*
Shopper in line:	*(Smiling broadly)* Two please.

For three or four more customers this pattern is repeated, then the salesperson pauses to look at the line again. He then looks behind him, back to the line and behind him again. He appears now to be counting how many people are in line compared to the amount of Zurphies he has left. After a few moments he walks over to the phone and calls someone. Everyone in the line is now focusing their attention on the salesperson as if trying to ascertain what he is saying or to whom he is talking. After a moment or two he nods his head and pushes another button on the phone. A click comes over the intercom and the unexcited voice of the salesperson soon follows.

Salesperson:	Attention all Zip Mart customers, due to the limited supply of Zurphie Robots, we can now only allow one per customer as long as supplies last. *(He pauses and a half smile comes over his face as those in the line begin to grumble)* Thank you for shopping at Zip Mart.
First lady:	*(Beginning to seem anxious)* Oh, if I don't get one of those, I don't know what I'll do. How long have we been in line anyway?
Second lady:	About twenty-five minutes.
First lady:	*(Seeming even more anxious)* And we're not even halfway up the line yet. I hope they have enough.
Second lady:	I'm sure they have plenty.

First lady: *(Standing on her tiptoes and craning around to see the salesperson)* I wish they would hurry up. I don't think this line is moving. *(Speaking loudly)* C-MON people, let's move it!

Second lady: *(Staring blankly at the first. She pats her on the back.)* It'll be okay, why don't you just enjoy the music.

Salesperson: *(From a distance)* Next.

First lady: *(Becoming more agitated)* "Enjoy the music," she says. I can't even hear myself talk over the music.

Second lady: Trust me, I can hear you just fine. We all can hear you just fine. *(A few people in the line agree)*

First lady: *(Her eyes light up and she smiles)* Hey, I got an idea. Why don't you run over there and pull the fire alarm. When everyone starts going outside, I'll run up and grab a Zurphie.

Second lady: Are you crazy?

First lady: *(Now she is completely distraught)* This is what I hate about Christmas. The crazy people getting all in the way. The crowds. Traffic. Those stupid blinky lights are starting to give me a headache. And the music. *(She grunts)* I can't even hear myself think over the music. *(The lights dim and the first lady's voice trails off)* Does this line ever move!

Scene 3:

The line is still long but the two ladies are almost to the front of the line. The first lady appears as if she is going to snap at any moment. An unnamed man enters the scene and is making his way forward along the side of the line, stopping and saying something to each person along the way. The line moves.

Second lady: *(Looking behind her)* I wonder what is going on back there. *(The unnamed man continues to make his way up the line. The line moves again and the two ladies are now third in line.)*

Salesperson: *(Hands a box to the next person in line and walks over to the phone on the wall and picks it up. Following a click he begins to speak. This time his voice seems to have some relief.)* Attention customers, we are now out of Zurphies.

First lady: *(Interrupts)* Oh no you're not! I stood in line for an hour and a half, you're gonna find me a Zurphie.

Salesperson: *(Continues while looking straight at the first lady)* But I have some good news.

First lady: If he tells me that he saved a bunch of money on his car insurance, I'm going to jump across that counter and choke him.

Salesperson: We still have a large number of the Zippy Robot in the toy section.

First lady: What's that? Does it do math or talk?

Salesperson: Uh, no. *(Through the commotion the unnamed man still makes his way through the line)*

First lady: Well, what does it do?

Salesperson: It walks and beeps.

First lady: *(Shakes her head and speaks aloud but as if she is talking to herself.)* "Walks and beeps," he says. Ha, ha. *(She laughs nervously.)* Walks and beeps. *(Her expression changes to anger as she lunges toward the salesperson)* I'm gonna . . . *(The second lady grabs her and holds her back. The first lady takes a deep breath.)* Okay, I'm fine. I'm fine. *(Everyone around is staring at her as if she were insane. At that moment someone comes by with a Zurphie. The first lady runs over and grabs it from the person and runs off. She madly runs toward the crowd that was once a long line. The unnamed man is still making his way through the crowd. The first lady looks back to see if she is being chased and runs into the unnamed man. Breathing heavily she looks at him with shock as he turns around.)*

Unnamed man: *(Smiles at her)* I just became a Christian and for the first time in my life I know the true meaning of Christmas. Do you? *(The first lady's face melts and tears well in her eyes as she realizes what she has become)*

A Christmas Readers' Theatre

Arranged by Kathy Murphy
and Jacqueline Rasar

Characters: -Readers 1 and 3, male
-Readers 2 and 4, female

Purpose: Christmas is a time of celebration and worship for the Christian. Through this comparison of Christ's humble birth and sacrificial death, hearts will be touched and lives challenged to honor God with a spirit of sincere celebration and worship.

Production: Set the stage for the four readers to address the audience. Be sure microphones are readily available and properly placed.

Props: None necessary

Length: 5 minutes

All: Joy to the world!

Reader 1: The Lord is come, let earth receive her King.

Reader 2: Tis the Lord, O wondrous story, tis the Lord . . .

All: The King of glory!

Reader 3: And it came to pass in those days, that there went out a decree from Caesar Augustus that all the world should be taxed . . .

Reader 1: The world in solemn stillness lay.

Reader 3: . . . and all went to be taxed, every one to his own city.

Reader 4: He came unto His own and His own received Him not.

Reader 3: Out of the city of Nazareth

Reader 4: Can any good thing come out of Nazareth?

Reader 3: Into Judea, unto the city of David, which is called Bethlehem. Behold there came wise men from the east to Jerusalem saying, "Where is He that is born King of the Jews?"

Reader 4: If thou be the King of the Jews "save thyself!"

Reader 3: For we have seen His star in the east and are come to worship Him.

Reader 2: The wise men sought to worship the Christ Child while King Herod sought to destroy Him.

Reader 3: And there were in the same country shepherds abiding in the fields keeping watch over their flocks by night. And lo, the angel of the Lord came upon them, and the glory of the Lord shown round about them.

All: And they were sore afraid.

Reader 3: And the angel said unto them, "Fear not, for behold, I bring you good tidings of great joy which shall be to all people."

Reader 1:   Hark! The herald angels sing,

Reader 2: Glory to the newborn King!

Reader 1:   Peace on earth and mercy mild

Reader 1 and 2:   God and sinners reconciled.

Reader 3:   For unto you is born this day . . .

Reader 4:   and shall be mocked . . .

Reader 3:   In the city of David . . .

Reader 4:   And spitefully entreated.

Reader 3:   A savior . . .

Reader 4:   And spit upon.

Reader 3:   Which is Christ the Lord.

Reader 4:   "Father, into thy hands I commend My spirit."

Reader 2:   Thou didst leave thy throne and thy kingly crown when thou camest to earth for me.

Reader 1:   Therefore, the Lord Himself will give you a sign, Behold; the virgin shall conceive and bear a son and shall call His name

Reader 2:   Emmanuel,

Reader 1 and 2:   God with us.

Reader 1:   With the name Emmanuel comes divine comfort.

Reader 2:   Christ was born for the purpose of sharing in the peril as well as the toil of our everyday lives.

Reader 1:   His desire is to empathize with us

Reader 1 and 2:   when we are hurting

Reader 1:   and to wipe the tears from our eyes.

Reader 1 and 2:   We can rejoice

Reader 2:   in the knowledge that God's Son, Jesus Christ, was born for the purpose of sharing in the joy as well as the laughter of our everyday lives.

Reader 1 and 2:   Born is the King of Israel!

Reader 1:   The image of Emmanuel becomes that of a man. Jesus wept,

Reader 2:   and rejoiced,

Reader 1:   He fasted . . .

Reader 2:   and feasted,

Reader 1 and 2:   and above all

Reader 1:   made Himself completely available to those He cherished,

Reader 2:   Emmanuel,

Reader 1 and 2:   God with us.

Reader 3:   And so it was that while they were there, the days were accomplished that she should be delivered.

Reader 4:   And having said this, He gave up the ghost.

Reader 1:   For to us a child is born, to us a Son is given

Reader 2:   Surely He has borne our griefs and carried our sorrows.

Reader 1 and 2:   The wonders of His love

Reader 3:   And she brought forth her firstborn son,

Reader 4:   And when Joseph had taken the body,

Reader 3:   And wrapped Him in swaddling clothes,

Reader 4:   And wrapped it in a clean linen cloth,

Reader 3:   And laid Him in a manger,

Reader 4:   And laid it in a tomb,

Reader 3:   Because there was no room for them in the inn.

Reader 4:   Wherein never man before was laid.

Reader 3:   And when they were come into the house,

Reader 4:   Upon the first day of the week,

Reader 3:   They saw the young child with Mary His mother.

Reader 4:   And they came unto the tomb.

Reader 1:   Be near me, Lord Jesus, I ask thee to stay close by me forever and love me I pray.

Reader 2:   O come to my heart, Lord Jesus, there is room in my heart for thee.

Reader 3:   And they presented unto Him gifts;

Reader 4:   Bringing the spices, which they had prepared;

Reader 1:   Present your gifts to Christ through prayer,

Reader 2:   worship,

Reader 1 and 2:   service,

Reader 3:   Gold, frankincense, and myrrh.

Reader 4:   They found the stone rolled away, behold two men stood by them in shining garments.

Reader 3:   And suddenly there was with the angel a multitude of the heavenly host,

Reader 4:   They said, "Why seek ye the living among the dead?"

Reader 3:   Glory to God in the highest!

Reader 4:   He is not here!

Reader 3:   And on earth, peace goodwill toward men!

Reader 4:   He is risen!

Reader 1:   Joy to the world!

Reader 2:   The savior reigns!

Reader 3:   Repeat the sounding joy.

Reader 1 and 2 and 4:   Joy to the world!

ALL: The Lord is come!

The Case of the Missing Christ

by Ammie Sullivent

Characters: -Jenny, cozy pajamas, journal, and pen
-Hugh DeMann, trench coat, hat, eyeglass, long list and pen
-Santa, Santa suit or red pants with suspenders, beard, and hat
-Mrs. Claus, dress and red apron, tray with cookies and mugs
-Peter Rabbit, rabbit ears and white sweat suit
-Grinch, green suit and spiked green hair
-Gingerbread Man, brown sweat suit trimmed like a gingerbread boy, jogging shoes
-Holly Wood, glamorous dress and high-heeled slippers
-Mrs. Mart, retail executive with business suit, professional look
-Mary, soft robe or wrap, baby doll wrapped in swaddling clothes
-Joseph, robe and walking stick

Purpose: No matter what the world makes of Christmas, it can never steal the truth. Christmas in the heart of a believer will always celebrate Christ, His birth, His life, His death, and resurrection.

Production: On one side of the stage set up a bedroom scene. Use a toddler bed or chairs for Jenny's bed. A small Christmas tree adds to the décor. The interviews will take place on the opposite side of the stage. Hugh's interviews with the Gingerbread Man could take place in the aisle if sound will permit.

Props: Bed, journal and pen, manger, long rolled-up list and pen, tray of cookies and mugs, Easter eggs, small paint brush, door, and character costuming

Length: 25-30 minutes

Scene 1:

Jenny: *(Writing out loud)* December 24—Today was like every other Christmas Eve: the big to-do at Grandma's house, lots of food, and presents from everyone. I don't know what I will do with all this stuff. I must admit I do love the gifts, even if Aunt Marge always gives me the wrong size. *(Starting to get tired, yawns and lies down on side and continues writing)* Tomorrow's the big day—Christmas! More food, more presents, and more family. It really feels like something is missing. I mean, we have a great tree with all the trimmings and tons of packages under it, but something is just not right. I've been told the story of Christmas a million times. I know we are supposedly celebrating the birth of Jesus, but when the day is over nothing has really changed. I do have a lot more stuff . . . but Jesus doesn't really come into the picture. *(Nodding off to sleep, Jenny questions)* What's missing? Where is Christ?

Hugh: *(Enters from stage left)* Jenny, wake up! I'm detective Hugh DeMann and I'm here to help you find the missing Christ.

Jenny: *(Drowsy and rubbing eyes)* What? You're De-Who?

Hugh: Hugh, Hugh DeMann, the greatest detective of all time.

Jenny: Why are you here? What's the problem?

Hugh: You said Christ was missing from Christmas. We must solve this crime and fast. You can't have Christmas without Christ.

Jenny: Well, actually, doesn't most of the world have Christmas without Christ? But sure I'll help. Where do we start?

Hugh: We start at the beginning, of course. You know the story. *(Mary and Joseph slowly walk across stage and place baby Jesus in manger. They look on the babe fondly and then walk off stage while Hugh continues speaking.)* The young Jewish girl named Mary found favor in the eyes of God. He chose her to bring His Son into this world. Mary and her new husband, Joseph, went to Bethlehem for the census. There were no rooms available so they stayed in a stable. That is when Jesus was born. Right there in the middle of the animals. Mary wrapped the babe in swaddling clothes and placed Him in a manger.

Jenny: Hugh, I am no time traveler. I cannot go back in time to the birth of the Christ child.

Hugh: Don't be silly, child. I know you can't go back. This is called retracing the steps. It will lead us to the solution of the case.

Jenny: So Jesus was there in the manger. Not missing yet!

Hugh: That's right! So we can cross off Mary and Joseph from the list of suspects. *(Pulls out long, rolled-up list from jacket and marks through the first names)* His childhood seems normal. No, no wait a minute. Jesus was missing after His family went to Jerusalem for the feast of the Passover.

Jenny: His family found Him in the temple, sitting among the teachers. He was listening and asking questions. Everyone was amazed at His understanding because He was just a boy.

Hugh: Yes, yes, that's right. He became a man and was baptized by John the Baptist. His ministry continued to show the love of God to all people. This angered the priests who judged the people according to their traditions. They had Jesus crucified. The perfect Lamb was hung on a cross to die for the sins of the whole world. That must be why He is missing. He was murdered. *(Sound effect . . . dun, dun, daaaa)*

Jenny: Mr. DeMann, Jesus rose from the dead. He defeated death and Satan. He gave us all a way back to God by taking on all of our sins. Jesus is alive.

Hugh: Back to the list. *(Pause and think)* It must be more recent. The abduction of Christ from Christmas must have just happened. I'll bet it's that Kris Kringle gent. I'll investigate. *(Walks slowly across stage as if walking a long time. Knocks on door. Santa opens it.)*

Santa: Ho, Ho, Ho! Welcome to the North Pole. Who do we have here?

Mrs. Claus: *(Quickly enters carrying a tray with cookies and cocoa)* Do we have visitors Kris? I made cookies and hot cocoa.

Santa: What can we do for you? Do you have a last minute request? Ho, Ho, Ho!

Mrs. Claus: Aren't you a tad too old to be asking for gifts from Santa?

Hugh: I'm Hugh, Hugh DeMann. I'm searching for Christ. He seems to be missing from Christmas.

Mrs. Claus: Well, what are you doing here? We wouldn't take Christ out of Christmas. We spread love and joy. The spirit of giving is what we're about.

Santa: Ho, Ho, Ho!

Hugh: But the focus of Christmas is taken away from Christ by all the gifts. The people say give me, give me, give me, more, more, more!

Mrs. Claus: Excuse me, Hugh DeMann. Is that the fault of the giver or the fault of the receiver?

Santa: Ho, Ho, Ho!

Hugh: Point taken. Thank you for your help and the cookie! *(Takes cookie and walks back to Jenny)*

Santa: Ho, Ho, Ho! *(Waving good-bye) (After Hugh leaves)* Put that one on the list of bad little boys.

Hugh: Scratch Ol' Saint Nick off the list of suspects. He is innocent. Maybe it's Peter Rabbit.

Jenny: Who's that?

Hugh: You know him better under his alias, "the Easter Bunny"! I'll be back. *(Walks back across stage)*

Peter Rabbit: *(Painting eggs)* Good day! May I help you, sir? I'm quite busy, millions of eggs to paint and just a few short months to get them done. I must work, but we can still talk. What do you need?

Hugh: Good day, Mr. Rabbit. I'm Hugh, Hugh DeMann. You're working awful hard for a holiday that is not really about you. Why do you do that?

Rabbit: I'm a hard working rabbit. I love to paint eggs. It's tradition.

Hugh: I'm on a mission. You see, tomorrow is Christmas and Christ is missing.

Rabbit: That's tragic, but I don't understand why you are here. I'm about Easter.

Hugh: I'm working on a jealousy theory. I thought you might want to rid the earth of Jesus so all the attention is turned to you at Easter.

Rabbit: Interesting theory I must say, but not accurate. You see, I take eggs to boys and girls all over the world. The eggs represent a new beginning. Without Christ in Christmas, the new beginning could never happen. Without Christ there is no Easter. Without Christ my job is gone, kaput, finished, over!

Hugh: I see what you're saying. Sorry to have wasted your time.

Rabbit: Have you tried the Grinch? I heard that he stole Christmas.

Hugh: Great idea! Thank you, Easter Bunny! (*Hugh walks back and forth across stage pretending to travel. Knocks on door. Grinch answers.*)

Grinch: Whom do we have here?

Hugh: Hugh, Hugh DeMann.

Grinch: Come in. I was about to eat breakfast. Would you like some? Would you like green eggs and ham?

Hugh: No thank you! I do not like green eggs and ham.

Grinch: Are you sure? We could eat them on the porch.

Hugh: I do not want them on the porch. I do not like green eggs and ham. I do not want to eat at all. I am here to talk, an important call.

Grinch: You must have come to get a fish. Which one would you like: red fish, blue fish, one fish, or two fish?

Hugh: I did not come to get a fish. If you would let me talk, you'd hear my wish. I've come to find the missing Christ and I've been told you're not too nice.

Grinch: I did not steal the Christ, you silly. I once stole Christmas from Ned and Nelly. I stole Christmas from WhoVille; I didn't steal Christ!

Hugh: So you stole Christmas. You're guilty, of course! It's your fault, you rotten horse.

Grinch: I'm not a horse and for your information, I returned Christmas to WhoVille and cheered the nation!

Hugh: So you didn't steal Christ from Christmas?

Grinch: You really need to listen. I did not take Him. I would not, could not steal the Christ. I suggest you check for some other heist.

Hugh: Thank you, Grinch, for no help at all. If you hear anything, give DeMann a call. *(Hugh walks back to the sleeping Jenny)*

Hugh: Jenny, wake up. Take the Easter Bunny and the Grinch off the list. They're not guilty at all if you get my gist.

Jenny: What's up with the rhyming?

Hugh: Oh, sorry. It's what happens when you talk to the Grinch.

Jenny: What about the Gingerbread Man? I hear he has quite the record! *(Gingerbread Man comes running across stage)* Look! There he is now!

Hugh: *(Takes off running after him, yelling)* Hey, wait for me! I have some questions for you! *(Hugh catches up to him for a minute)* I know you have a track record. Do you have anything to say about Christ missing from Christmas?

Gingerbread Man: My track record's for speed, not stealing. *(Gingerbread Man picks up speed and yells back to Hugh)* You can't catch me, you can't catch me 'cause I'm the Gingerbread Man. *(Hugh is exhausted and pants hard. He turns and walks back to Jenny with his hand over his chest.)*

Hugh: It's not the Gingerbread Man. He is focused on his running. Wow, is he fast! *(Hugh sits on the edge of the bed and hangs his head as if he is tired)*

Jenny: Maybe it's Holly Wood. She steals all kinds of stuff from our pure, innocent hearts. She doesn't want people to know about Christ.

Hugh: Great idea, Jenny. I shall return.

Hugh: *(Travels across stage. Meets Holly Wood, walking with an attitude)* Hello there, Miss. Are you Holly Wood?

Holly: I am. How did you know?

Hugh: I could tell by your attitude. I'm investigating a missing person report. Christ has been taken from Christmas. I believe you might have something to do with it.

Holly: Me, you must be insane. I don't take people. I simply tell stories.

Hugh: Holly, you know better than that. You take stories and twist them out of shape, distorting the truth to where it becomes something totally different. You take morals and corrupt them. You lie to the youth about what's right and wrong. You are disgusting and selfish. Am I wrong?

Holly: *(Hands over face, sobbing dramatically like a diva actress)* You're right! I'm horrible, but I didn't steal Christ. Try the retail executives. They steal everything right out of your wallet.

Hugh: Don't cast the blame. Take charge of your life.

Holly: I'm sorry! I'm sorry! But I didn't steal Christ.

Hugh: Fine, but if you hear anything . . . give DeMann a call! *(Walks away)*

Hugh: *(Calls Jenny and tells her that he is on his way to talk to the retail executives)* Mrs. Mart? You must know by now that Christ is missing from Christmas. Are you the responsible party?

Mrs. Mart: You must be crazy . . . Haven't you figured it out? You are a worthless detective. The retail execs would not take Christ out of Christmas. Without the true meaning of Christmas, the giving would stop. We would make no money. What would be the point?

Hugh: You don't have to be so harsh. I'm just checking all sources and I came down to you.

Mart: If Christ is missing from Christmas, might I suggest your own heart?

Hugh: My heart has nothing to do with it. Jenny is the one that said Christ was missing and that Christmas changes nothing.

Mart: Then I would check with Jenny. Tell her to examine her own heart.

Hugh: I think you are on to something. I appreciate your help. Merry Christmas, Mrs. Mart.

Hugh: *(Walks back to Jenny)* Jenny, are you sleeping again? Wake up; we must check this one out together!

Jenny: What do you mean? You're the great detective. You figure it out.

Hugh: I think I might have solved the case. But first I must ask you a few questions.

Jenny: Me, why me? I have nothing to do with it.

Hugh: You said that Christmas changes nothing.

Jenny: That's right. It all goes back to the same old thing, day after day, nothing new.

Hugh: How do you treat other people, Jenny?

Jenny: I really don't think about other people, unless I need something.

Hugh: Do you love others as you love yourself?

Jenny: They are not as lovable as me.

Hugh: Jenny, what did you just say?

Jenny: I'm sorry. That sounds really bad, doesn't it?

Hugh: Jenny, do you love the Lord with all your heart, soul, mind, and strength?

Jenny: Of course, I love God. I go to church every Sunday. I even watch the babies in the nursery sometimes. If the church is lucky I will sing in the choir or even sing a solo.

Hugh: That's not loving God. That is performing. Do you really know God? Do you spend time with Him daily in prayer? Do you read the love letter He provides for you? Jenny, you must take up your cross daily. Die to yourself and live for Christ. Serve others. Show the love that Christ was born to show. No wonder everything is the same after Christmas . . . . You must live Christ every minute.

Jenny: So I stole Christ from Christmas.

Hugh: All fingers point to you. *(All characters gather around Jenny and point a finger at her)* Jenny, you are the only one that can accept Christ or deny Christ. No one else can do that for you. You must make the choice. Once you accept Jesus as your Lord and Savior, you will never suffer from another case of the missing Christ. He will never leave you.

Jenny: Oh Hugh, you really are DeMann. Thank you for opening my eyes! I've been so selfish. I choose Christ. *(Hugh and all characters exits stage left and Jenny lies back down)*

Jenny: *(Waking Christmas morning, looking around)* Hugh, where did you go? That must have been a dream. *(Jenny stands up and yells, running off stage)* Mom, Dad, wake up, it's Christmas! Jesus was born today to save the world. We are His hands and feet. God wants us to tell everyone that Jesus Christ is born! Wake up! Wake up! We have a mission to do!!!

Name That Tradition

by Suzanne Hadley

Characters: Game show host
Candy Cane, female
Chris Kringle, male
Fa Lalalala, male

Purpose: To provide the history of and meaning behind popular Christmas traditions, including those with spiritual significance. This skit will challenge viewers to look past the frivolity and fun of Christmas to the reason we celebrate.

Production: Set the stage for a game show with three contestants

Props: Music and player, three pieces of paper and markers, question cards for host

Length: 5-7 minutes

Scene 1:

Host: Hello and welcome to "Name That Tradition," the show where average people come up with the meanings behind popular holiday traditions. We're glad you could join us. I'd like to call our first contestant. Candy Cane, come on down! *(Commotion as Candy comes down) (Host, clearing throat)* All right, good to have you on the show, Candy. Let's get our next contestant down here. Chris Kringle, come on down! Welcome to the show! And our final contestant is . . . Fa Lalalala? *(Fa comes down)* That's an interesting name.

Fa: It's short for Fabio.

Host: Okay. Welcome.

Our first question is for Candy. Where did the tradition begin of Santa Claus, a man in a red suit giving out toys to children?

Candy: The North Pole?

Host: Ooo. I'm sorry. That is incorrect. It began in Turkey during the 4th century. Saint Nicholas devoted his life to Christianity and became known for his generosity and love for children.

Candy: That's what I meant.

Host: Okay. Next question is for Chris. Where did we first hear about Rudolph the Red-Nosed Reindeer pulling Santa's sleigh?

Chris: That's easy. It all began one foggy Christmas Eve, when Santa came to say, "Rudolph with your nose so bright, won't you guide my sleigh tonight?"

Host: Is that your final answer?

Chris: You betcha!

Host: Wrong. Rudolph was actually invented by Robert L. May, who wrote the story of Rudolph as a promotion for the Montgomery Ward company. It was later set to music and recorded by Gene Autry in 1949.

Chris: I can't believe this! It's all about commercialism? I feel so betrayed!

Host: Moving on . . . Fa, why do we give fruitcakes to one another for Christmas?

Fa: Um, er, um. I don't know.

Host: *(Looking at answer card and throwing it over shoulder)* Neither do we. How about a different question? Why do we bring Christmas trees into our homes during the holidays?

Fa: Oh, no way! I know this one. It's to drive out that bachelor smell with fresh pine. I can actually invite girls over to the house at Christmas.

Crowd person: *(Presumably friend)* Yeah, Dude!

Host: No, I'm sorry, it's not for the fresh pine scent—*(turning to audience)* although that is very nice. In ancient times people brought evergreen branches into their homes to symbolize life. They believed the branches scared away demons. Later, they added candles to represent Christ, the Light of the World. Back to Candy. Why do people give gifts to one another on Christmas?

Candy: Um, oohhh, uh, I know this. Hang on. *(Chris is squirming like he knows the answer)* Um, doesn't it have something to do with Santa? Or maybe Frosty the Snowman. No, wait—it's Santa. He started giving presents to his reindeer and . . .

Host: No, I'm sorry. That is incorrect. People give gifts to remember the wise men's gifts to the Christ child.

Chris: I knew that! *(Gets a dirty look from Candy)*

Host: Chris. It's your turn. How did the tradition of caroling begin?

Chris: Well, I think it was like trick-or-treating. People realized they didn't have to wait until Halloween to get goodies from their neighbors, so they started going door to door to get stuff like, um, eggnog or waffles. And then, so they wouldn't have to stay very long, they would sing songs, like, um, *(singing off-key)* "We wish you a merry Christmas, we wish you a merry Christmas, we wish you a merry Christmas . . . ."

Host: Whoa! Stop! That's incorrect.

Chris: *(Singing)* "And a happy new year!"

Host: The correct answer is that early carols were cheerful circle dances and songs about Christ, Christians used to celebrate the joy of Advent. Going door-to-door came later. Now a question for Fa. Why do we set up small nativity scenes in our houses?

Fa: Interesting you should ask. I think, um, it's to give us that old-fashioned, nostalgic feeling. With the angels and sheep and cows and stuff.

Host: Not exactly . . . Nativity scenes are also called *crèches*, which is the French word for manger. Saint Francis of Assisi set up a famous crèche *(kresh)* in the Italian town of Grecio in the 13th century. At that time churches displayed mangers at Christmas covered with gold, silver, and jewels. Saint Francis thought it was important for people to remember that Christ was born in a simple stable. So he gathered people and animals together in a cave on Christmas Eve. They acted out the story of the first Christmas by candlelight. Hmm. Our contestants don't seem to be doing so well. Lucky for them, there's a bonus round. For our bonus round we will ask all three contestants the same question. A correct answer wins the game! Traditionally, what were the names of the three wise men who visited Jesus? *(Game show music plays as contestants write their answers)*

Host: Candy?

Candy: *(Holds up sign)* Dasher, Dancer, and Comet.

Host: I'm sorry. That's incorrect. Chris?

Hunter: *(Holds up sign)* Scrooge, Marley, and the Grinch.

Host: I'm sorry, but that's not right either. Fa?

Fa: *(Holds up sign)* Gaspar, Melchior, and Balthasar.

Host: *(Gasping)* That's right! How did you know?

Fa: Oh, just a lucky guess.

Host: Great job. I'd like to thank all our contestants for being on "Name That Tradition." Fa will receive an all-expense paid vacation to the North Pole.

Fa: Yes! It's what I've always wanted.

Host: And as a parting gift, each of you in our studio audience will receive a fruitcake. Happy Holidays! *(Ending music)*

The Christmas Child

by Pamela G. Johnson

Characters: -Narrator
-Father
-Mother
-Mariah, a girl 7-9 years old
-Joseph
-Mary
-Crowd consists of 3 people, any age
-Doll's voice, offstage

Purpose: This skit helps us understand the deep, unconditional love God shows in giving us the gift of His Son. Even though He knew this precious gift would be rejected by many, He sent His Son anyway. The world needs to know and appreciate the sacrifice our Father made for each one of us.

Production: Stage Right is a living room with a couch, table, and Christmas tree with presents under it. Stage Left is a nativity set with a manger.

Props: Table with doll making tools, etc., homemade girl doll, gift bag with tissue paper, Christmas tree with wrapped presents under it, manger with hay, doll for use as Baby Jesus, modern clothes for family and crowd, biblical period attire for Joseph and Mary, lights for Stage Left and Stage Right that can be dimmed on cue.

Length: 9-10 minutes

Scene 1:

Stage Right: Stage is dark. Lights come on Father standing at a table adding finishing touches to a doll he has made. He is humming "Away in a Manger."

Father: *(Holds doll up to look at it)* There, I'm just about done. *(Talking to the doll)* Oh yes, Mariah is going to love you. She will take one look at you and her heart will melt. You are so much better than the one she saw at the mall. The one she *thinks* she wants. The one she thinks will make her happy. You aren't some assembly line doll like that one, with a blank stare and a fake smile. You aren't what the toy stores created.

Narrator: *(Spotlight stays on the father working on the doll during the narration)*

"Beloved, do not believe every spirit, but test the spirits to see whether they are from God, because many false prophets have gone out into the world." *(1 John 4:1)*

(Note: The Scripture reference is given for reference only if the Reader wishes to use another translation. Scripture reference is not meant to be read aloud by Reader.)

"They are from the world; therefore they speak as from the world, and the world listens to them." *(1 John 4:5)*

"See to it that no one takes you captive through philosophy and empty deception, according to the tradition of men, according to the elementary principles of the world, rather than according to Christ." *(Colossians 2:8)*

Father: *(Still speaking to the doll)* I do hope Mariah sees and understands how much love and sacrifice I put into creating you, the perfect gift. You are custom made. You are made just for Mariah. I hope she notices the little details like your eyes are the same color as hers, and your dress matches her favorite dress. And oh, when she hugs you. *(Pleading with the unseen girl)* Oh please, Mariah, embrace this doll so you'll know and understand the love I put into this gift just for you.

Narrator: *(Spotlight stays on Father admiring the doll)* "For God so loved the world, that He gave His only begotten Son, that whoever believes in Him shall not perish, but have eternal life. For God did not send the Son into the world to judge the world, but that the world might be saved through Him." *(John 3:16, 17)*

Lights go down on Father, come up on the nativity scene Stage Left. Joseph and Mary are kneeling by a manger gazing with love at their child lying in the hay.

Joseph: *(Quoting Matthew 1:20, 21)* "An angel of the Lord appeared to him in a dream, saying, 'Joseph, son of David, do not be afraid to take Mary as your wife; for the Child who has been conceived in her is of the Holy Spirit. And she will bear a Son; and you shall call His name Jesus, for He will save His people from their sins.'"

Mary: *(Quoting Luke 2:6, 7)* "While they were there the days were completed for her to give birth. And she gave birth to her first-born son; and she wrapped Him in cloths, and laid Him in a manger, because there was no room for them in the inn."

Joseph: *(Quoting Isaiah 9:6)* "For a child will be born to us, a son will be given to us; And the government will rest on His shoulders; And His name will be called Wonderful Counselor, Mighty God, Eternal Father, Prince of Peace."

Mary: *(Quoting Luke 2:8, 9)* "In the same region there were some shepherds staying out in the fields and keeping watch over their flock by night. And an angel of the Lord suddenly stood before them, and the glory of the Lord shone around them; and they were terribly frightened."

Joseph: *(Quoting Luke 2:10, 11)* "But the angel said to them, 'Do not be afraid; for behold, I bring you good news of great joy which will be for all the people; for today in the city of David there has been born for you a Savior, who is Christ the Lord.'"

Mary: *(Quoting Luke 2:12)* "This will be a sign for you: you will find a baby wrapped in cloths and lying in a manger."

Lights fade on nativity scene, come up Stage Right on living room scene. The mother is sitting on the couch; father and child are sitting in front of a Christmas tree. The girl is about to open her doll as the father and mother watch in happy anticipation.

Mariah: *(Excitedly pulling out the doll from the gift bag. She looks at her, and her expression abruptly changes from one of pure joy to one of bitter disappointment. She becomes angry.)* This isn't the right doll! It's not the one I saw at the mall that all my friends have! *(Throws the doll on the ground and glares at her father)* I hate it! I won't accept your gift! *(The father is crestfallen. The family freezes.)*

Lights stay on family; lights come up on the nativity scene where Mary and Joseph are standing. Mary is holding the "child" protectively. A crowd of three has gathered around them.

Person 1: *(Mockingly)* A baby? Born in a manger? Just a nobody?

Person 2: *(Sarcastically)* The Savior of the world? I think not!

Person 3: *(Bitterly)* We won't accept this Child as our King . . .

All: We hate this Child! *(Glare angrily at Mary and Joseph)*

All: We reject Him! *(Glare heavenward and shake fists at God)*

Major pause; everyone freezes. Lights stay up on both sets during narration.

Narrator: "For He grew up before Him like a tender shoot, And like a root out of parched ground; He has no stately form or majesty That we should look upon Him, Nor appearance that we should be attracted to Him. He was despised and forsaken of men, A man of sorrows, and acquainted with grief; and like one from whom men hide their face He was despised, and we did not esteem Him." *(Isaiah 53:2, 3)*

Lights fade on the nativity scene, but stay up on the family. Father carefully picks up the doll, gets off the floor and sits on the couch, then lovingly gathers Mariah into his lap. The mother looks on expectantly, maybe caressing the child's hair.

Father: *(Quietly and lovingly)* Mariah, what do you think makes something special? *(She shrugs)* When it is made especially for you and when it is given in love. The dolls in the mall weren't made with any love. In fact, they probably weren't even touched by human hands. They were made by machines. We only want those dolls because the world tells us we want and need them. How much better is one made just for you by loving hands. Look at her eyes, Mariah. *(Mariah hesitantly inspects the eyes)* Look at her dress. *(Mariah smoothes it down and smiles with recognition)* She is a special doll . . . made just for you. *(The family freezes.)*

Lights stay up on the family, come up on Stage Left. Mary and Joseph are still standing with the crowd. Mary is holding the child.

Narrator: "But God demonstrates His own love toward us, in that while we were yet sinners, Christ died for us. Much more then, having now been justified by His blood, we shall be saved from the wrath of God through Him. For if while we were enemies we were reconciled to God through the death of His Son, much more, having been reconciled, we shall be saved by His life." *(Romans 5:8-10)*

Person 1:   *(Comprehending it)* "For the wages of sin is death, but the free gift of God is eternal life in Christ Jesus our Lord." *(Romans 6:23)*

Person 2:   *(Gathering the child into his arms from Mary)* The stone which the builders rejected has become the chief corner stone. *(Ps 118:22)*

Narrator: "I am the good shepherd, and I know My own and My own know Me, even as the Father knows Me and I know the Father; and I lay down My life for the sheep." *(John 10:14, 15)*

"and the sheep hear his voice, and he calls his own sheep by name . . ." *(John 10:3)*

Lights fade on the nativity scene.

Father: This doll is a special gift, made with my heart and soul just for you. She wants you to love and accept her. (*Handing Mariah the doll*) Hug her. (*Mariah is reluctant*) Go ahead, embrace the doll. (*She hugs the doll*)

Doll: I love you, Mariah.

Mariah: (*Looks startled, then questioningly at the father*) She said my name. How does she know my name?

Father: (*Smiling happily and knowingly at Mariah*) Because that is how she is designed.

Mariah joyfully hugs the doll again.

Doll: I love you, Mariah.

Lights fade out.

Down From His Glory

by Kenneth Carr

Characters: -Father
-Mother
-Children of varied ages, gathered around and/or sitting on parents' laps
-One or more singers
-Reader, preferably man with good speaking voice

Purpose: "Down From His Glory" was written to meet the need of a small country church for a Christmas program. In order to involve as many people as possible, especially young people, and to reduce rehearsal times, this format—something fresh and unusual—was developed. Of course, conveyance of the gospel message and the endeavor to gain personal reception of the message by both performers and audience were of paramount importance.

Production: Stage should appear to be a family's living room during the Christmas season

Props: Living room sitting (chairs, couch, recliner, etc.), tables, lamps, bookshelves, greenery—any props to make stage a convincing living room setting

Length: 12-15 minutes

Reader: *(Speaks from behind curtain, or down in front off the stage)* Christmas is a special time when Christian families get together around the Word of God. This family on the stage represents what might happen in your home and mine sometime during the Christmas season.

Father: Once upon a time, God up in heaven sent His only Son down to earth, down from the riches and glories of heaven, to be born a tiny baby to the home of poor people, Mary and Joseph.

Singer: *(From behind curtain, or down in front off the stage)* "Down From His Glory," p. 12, #2 *Favorites*, verse 1 ("Down from His glory, Ever living story, My God and Savior came, and Jesus was His name; Born in a manger to His own a stranger, A man of sorrows, tears and agony! Oh how I love Him! How I adore Him! My breath, my sunshine, my all in all! The great Creator became my Savior, And all God's fullness dwelleth in Him!")

Reader: "God, who is rich in mercy, for his great love wherewith he loved us, Even when we were dead in sins, . . . hath raised us up together, . . . That in the ages to come he might shew the exceeding riches of his grace . . . toward us through Christ Jesus." *(Ephesians 2:4-7)* "For by grace are ye saved through faith; and that not of yourselves: it is the gift of God: Not of works, lest any man should boast." *(Ephesians 2:8, 9)*

(Note: The Scripture reference is given for reference only if the Reader wishes to use another translation. Scripture reference is not meant to be read aloud by Reader.)

Singer: "Down From His Glory," verse 2 ("What condescension, Bringing us redemption, That in the dead of night, Not one faint hope in sight, God gracious, tender Laid aside His splendor, Stooping to woo, To win, to save my soul! Oh how I love Him! How I adore Him! My breath, my sunshine, my all in all! The great Creator became my Savior, And all god's fullness dwelleth in Him!")

Reader: "For ye know the grace of our Lord Jesus Christ, that, though he was rich, yet for your sakes he became poor, that ye through his poverty might be rich." *(2 Corinthians 8:9)*

Singer: "Down From His Glory," verse 3 ("Without reluctance, Flesh and blood His substance, He took the form of man, Revealed the hidden plan; O glorious myst'ry Sacrifice of Calv'ry! And now I know He is the great 'I AM'! Oh how I love Him! How I adore Him! My breath, my sunshine, my all in all! The great Creator became my Savior, And all God's fullness dwelleth in Him!")

Father: The night Christ was born, angels came down from heaven to tell the news to some shepherds who were watching their sheep out in the country near Bethlehem.

Reader: "It came to pass, as the angels were gone away from them into heaven, the shepherds said one to another, Let us now go even unto Bethlehem, and see this thing which is come to pass, which the Lord hath made known unto us. And they came with haste, and found Mary, and Joseph, and the babe lying in a manger. And when they had seen it, they made known abroad the saying which was told them concerning this child. And all they that heard it wondered at those things which were told them by the shepherds . . . . And the shepherds returned, glorifying and praising God for all the things that they had heard and seen, as it was told unto them." *(Luke 2:15-18, 20)*

Father: Mary and Joseph took the baby Jesus to the temple when he was 8 days old. There, two very old people saw Him. They had been hoping for many years to see Him.

Singer: "It Came Upon the Midnight Clear," verse 4 ("For lo, the days are hastening on, By prophet bards foretold, When with the ever-circling years Comes round the age of gold; When peace shall over all the earth Its ancient splendors fling, And the whole world give back the song Which now the angels sing.") (Edmund H. Sears, *Rejoice*, pg 140)

Reader: "And, behold, there was a man in Jerusalem, whose name was Simeon; and the same man was just and devout, waiting for the consolation of Israel: and the Holy Ghost was upon him. And it was revealed unto him by the Holy Ghost, that he should not see death, before he had seen the Lord's Christ. And he came by the Spirit into the temple: and when the parents brought in the child Jesus, to do for him after the custom of the law, Then took he him up in his arms, and blessed God, and said, Lord, now lettest thou thy servant depart in peace, according to thy word: For mine eyes have seen thy salvation." *(Luke 2:25-30)*

Singer: "Angels From the Realms of Glory," verse 4 ("Saints before the altar bending , Watching long in hope and fear, Suddenly the Lord descending, In His temple shall appear: Come and worship, come and worship, Worship Christ, the new-born King. Amen.") (James Montgomery, *Rejoice*, pg 135)

Reader: "There was one Anna, a prophetess . . . of a great age. . . . She was a widow of about fourscore and four years, which departed not from the temple, but served God with fastings and prayers night and day. And she coming in that instant gave thanks likewise unto the Lord, and spake of him to all them that looked for redemption in Jerusalem." *(Luke 2:36-38)*

Father: Over in an eastern country, far away from Bethlehem, some wise men had been watching the sky. They watched every night for a long time. They were expecting a new star to shine. They knew it would be a sign that Jesus Christ, the Messiah, had come to earth.

Singer: "Angels From the Realms of Glory," verse 3 ("Wise men, leave your contemplation, Brighter visions beam afar; Seek the great Desire of nations, Ye have seen His natal star: Come and worship, come and worship, Worship Christ, the new-born King. Amen.")

Reader: "Now when Jesus was born in Bethlehem of Judaea in the days of Herod the king, behold, there came wise men from the east to Jerusalem, Saying, Where is he that is born King of the Jews? for we have seen his star in the east, and are come to worship him. When Herod the king had heard these things, he was troubled, and all Jerusalem with him. And when he had gathered all the chief priests and scribes of the people together, he demanded of them where Christ should be born. And they said unto him, In Bethlehem of Judaea: for thus it is written by the prophet." *(Matthew 2:1-5)*

Singer: "As With Gladness Men of Old," verses 1 and 2 ("As with gladness men of old, Did the guiding star behold, As with joy they hailed its light, Leading onward, beaming bright, So, most glorious Lord, may we Evermore be led to Thee" and "As with joyous steps they sped, To that lowly manger bed, There to bend the knee before Him, Whom heaven and earth adore; So may we with willing feet Ever seek Thy mercy seat.") (Dix and Kocher, *Worship and Service Hymnal,* pg 28)

Father: When Jesus was about twelve years old, the family traveled from their home in Galilee. They went to Jerusalem for the feast of the Passover. It was on this trip they were reminded that Jesus was the Son of God.

Reader: "And when he was twelve years old, they went up to Jerusalem after the custom of the feast. And when they had fulfilled the days, as they returned, the child Jesus tarried behind in Jerusalem; and Joseph and his mother knew not of it. But they, supposing him to have been in the company, went a day's journey; and they sought him among their kinsfolk and acquaintance. And when they found him not, they turned back again to Jerusalem, seeking him. And it came to pass, that after three days they found him in the temple, sitting in the midst of the doctors, both hearing them, and asking them questions. And all that heard him were astonished at his understanding and answers . . . And Jesus increased in wisdom and stature, and in favour with God and man." *(Luke 2:42-47, 52)*

Father: People liked Jesus, even when He was a child. He was good and obedient in the home.

Singer: "Tell Me the Stories of Jesus," verse 1 ("Tell me the stories of Jesus I love to hear; Things I would ask Him to tell me If He were here: Scenes by the wayside, Tales of the sea, Stories of Jesus, Tell them to me.") (William H. Parker, *Rejoice,* 152)

Father: The next thing the Bible tells about Jesus is when He was 30 years old and began His ministry. He taught His disciples. He preached to great crowds. He healed people and did many miracles. Then he shed His precious blood on the cross for us, died and rose again. Now He lives in heaven and is preparing a home there for those who love Him.

Reader: "Jesus said, 'I go to prepare a place for you. And if I go and prepare a place for you, I will come again, and receive you unto myself; that where I am, there ye may be also.'" *(John 14:2, 3)*

Father: And that's the story of Christmas.

Singer: "Have You Any Room for Jesus?" verses 1 and 4 ("Have you any room for Jesus, He who bore your load of sin? As He knocks and asks admission, Sinner, will you let Him in? Room for Jesus, King of glory! Hasten now, His word obey; Swing your heart's door widely open, Bid Him enter while you may." and "Room and time now give to Jesus, Soon will pass God's day of grace ; Soon thy heart left cold and silent, And thy Savior's pleading cease. Room for Jesus, King of glory! Hasten now, His word obey; Swing your heart's door widely open, Bid Him enter while you may.") (Unknown, *Rejoice*, 256)

The Christmas Letter

by Kaye Brooks

Characters: -Howard, age 65 or over, father of Melody and Adam
-Melody, age 40-45
-Jim, age 40-45, Melody's husband
-Adam, age 35-40
-Susan, age 35-40, Adam's wife
-Zack, age 16-20, son of Melody and Jim
-Amanda, age 8-12, daughter of Adam and Susan
-Marjorie (Mom), age 65+, dressed in a simple white robe or gown

Purpose: Christmas is a time for celebration, but when the circumstances in our lives are trying and full of grief, it's difficult to celebrate. Yet, as Christians, we are to take our eyes off circumstances and look fully in the wonderful face of Jesus. We are not as those who have no hope. We have the blessed hope of Jesus, which gives us reason to celebrate and offer praise even in the worst of circumstances. The purpose of this script is to encourage all of us to remember that Christmas is not just about the birth of a baby, but the birth of hope, joy, and new life in Christ.

Production: Stage should be set up as a living room

Props: living room furniture (use whatever is available to you and will fit into the space you have), Christmas tree (real or artificial), Christmas wreath, garland, Christmas decorations packed in storage boxes, letter (inside one of the boxes)

Length: 10 minutes

Scene 1:

It is the first Saturday evening of December. The whole family has gotten together for their traditional dinner (and Christmas decorating), but no one except Howard and the kids are in the mood to celebrate Christmas.

(Melody, Jim, Adam and Susan enter the living room after dinner.)

Adam: *(Rubbing his stomach)* Great dinner, Sis! *(Reflectively)* You certainly inherited Mom's gift for cooking.

Melody: It's so strange cooking in Mom's kitchen without her. Even when the chemo made her too weak to stand, she'd sit at the table and keep me company while I cooked.

Jim: *(Trying to comfort her)* She was still there with you, honey—in spirit.

Melody: *(Sighing)* I still can't believe she's gone.

Susan: It's only been two months. I've heard that this is the *really* rough time. The shock wears off, sympathy cards stop coming, the world gets back to normal—except for yours—and now with the holidays . . . it's just so hard.

Melody: Thanksgiving was difficult enough. I mean, I'm thankful Mom's no longer in pain, and I know she's healthy and whole again in heaven . . . but I miss her so much. *(Cries softly)* I just don't think I can make it through Christmas.

Adam: Yeah, I know. Mom always made Christmas so special. It's just not going to be the same without her. *(Chuckles)* Remember how she'd always pull out those Santa mugs with our names on them for the eggnog every year?

Melody: *(Laughs a little)* Oh, yes, even as adults. Her excuse was that the names kept everybody's drinks straight. I think she really did it to help pull out the child in each of us.

Adam: It worked! But then, Mom had that effect on people. She was like a child at Christmas. I think it was just contagious.

Susan: She made every member of the family a special tapestry stocking to hang on the mantle—each one with a scene from the nativity. I remember when she gave me my stocking the first year Adam and I were married. It had a beautiful sparkling angel on it and she told me I was Adam's angel. *(Sniffs)* She made me feel like I was really her daughter, not a daughter-in-law.

Melody: I would sometimes get so tired and frustrated with her when we would go Christmas shopping together. She had to have the perfect gift for everyone and we would go from store to store until she found it. It didn't have to be expensive, in fact it usually wasn't, but it had to be special. Sometimes I just wanted to shout, "Just pick something—anything!" Then, when she did find that perfect gift, her eyes would light up with such joy . . . it was those times that really taught me the meaning of "It is more blessed to give, than to receive."

Jim: I wonder how many bags of flour she went through baking all her Christmas goodies for friends and neighbors? *(Playfully nudges Adam)* We'd spend a whole Saturday out with your dad delivering your mom's Christmas care packages.

Adam: Yeah, all with a note that read, "Merry Christmas with love from Jesus and the Cranstons." *(Pause, fighting back tears)* Maybe this year we ought to keep Christmas low key. You know, not do a lot of decorating, cut back on gifts, maybe even go out for Christmas dinner—do something we've never done before.

Jim: That would certainly take the stress off everybody.

Susan: I think that's a good idea for *us*, but I don't know how Zack and Amanda are going to feel about it—or your dad. He and your mom have always gone all out for Christmas.

Adam: I think Dad just went along with Mom's plans 'cause she enjoyed Christmas so much. And the kids . . . well a little dose of reality will help them to appreciate what they have. It'll do them good.

Melody: *(Realizes Howard, Zack, and Amanda are not with them)* Speaking of Dad and the kids . . . where are they?

Adam: I thought they were in the kitchen cleaning up. *(Everyone looks at him with a "you've got to be kidding" look)* OK . . . crazy idea.

Howard: *(Off stage)* Just take everything into the living room. *(Zack enters with boxes of Christmas decorations. Amanda is carrying a wreath and has garland draped around her neck. Howard follows with a Christmas tree.)*

Melody: Dad! What are you doing? You're not planning on decorating now are you?

Howard: Of course I am. This is the first Saturday of December. It's tradition! *(Melody, Jim, Adam, and Susan look at each other awkwardly.)*

Adam: Dad . . . we were just talking about maybe keeping things a little low key this year . . . you know, not do much decorating and . . . stuff . . .

Howard: Nonsense! We *need* to do this.

Melody: Dad, I don't know if I can! *(Pause)* I miss Mom so much.

Howard: *(Goes to Melody and comforts her)* I know, Princess . . . I know. I miss her too. But I'm sure she wants us to celebrate just as much as we usually do.

Jim: You speak of her as if she were still alive.

Howard: That's because she *is* alive. *(Everyone else looks at each other thinking, "Oh boy, he's really lost it!")* We haven't *lost* Marjorie. We know exactly where she is—she's in heaven—and I can guarantee you, she's going to be celebrating

Melody: But, Dad . . .

Howard: No buts, not celebrating Christmas would disrespect your mother . . . and more important . . . it would disrespect Jesus.

Susan: What do you mean?

Howard: When Marjorie was diagnosed with cancer, we went to the Bible for comfort. One verse in particular jumped out at us—1 Thessalonians 4:13: "Brothers, we do not want you to be ignorant about those who fall asleep, or to grieve like the rest of men, who have no hope." Yes, we miss her, but we have the hope that Jesus brings. We know that because of Jesus, we will be reunited one day.

Adam: You're right Dad. I'm sorry I even made the suggestion.

Melody: *(Half-heartedly)* Well then, let's get started. But I think we'd better get a box of tissues ready for the tears that are bound to flow.

Zack: *(Zack opens the box of decorations and finds a letter on top. With a puzzled expression he lifts it out of the box.)* There's a letter in the decorations. It's addressed to "My beloved family."

Amanda: *(Takes letter out of Zack's hand)* It's Grandma's handwriting. *(She hands the letter to Howard and he opens it)*

Howard: *(Reading)* My dear ones, if you are reading this, *(Marjorie enters unseen by the other characters, Howard and Marjorie speak together)* you have at least managed to open the box of Christmas decorations this year.

Marjorie: *(Howard continues to mouth the words, but only Marjorie is speaking. Marjorie moves among them as she speaks, but they react only to Howard as he reads the letter)* Howard, my love, I am sure that you are the one that insisted on decorating against the protests of our grieving children. I know they love you so much and want to protect everyone from the pain. And I am sure that by now, you have shared with them the verse that came to mean so much to us during my illness, 1 Thessalonians 4:13. I know all of you miss me. It's only natural to miss the ones we love when they go away. But, as Christians, we never have to say good-bye, only, 'til we meet again."

I have been called home for Christmas this year! Rejoice with me in this! I will be celebrating with Jesus Himself this year. And, this will be the first Christmas I get to celebrate with Jonathan, our baby that was called home even before he was born. I have your whole lifetimes to tell him about and catch him up on his wonderful family he never got to know.

Amanda, you have always been a good girl, not perfect—but good. I am so thankful that you made the decision to accept Christ as your Lord and Savior while I was still with you. That was the greatest gift you could ever give me. As you approach your teen years remember to put Jesus first—above friends, boys, school, and other activities. Listen to and obey your parents. And, I pray that when you are all grown up, you will be a wonderful young woman just like your mom. May God's grace always shine on you and through you, my beautiful child.

Zack, I could not have asked for a better grandson. You are a fine young man, even though you were a little terror in your early years! Your parents, Grandpa, and I would take turns going to the church nursery when one of the teachers would come to get us to calm you down. It would have been very easy for your parents to give up on church and stay home with you— but they didn't. They kept you in Sunday School and it paid off. I'll never forget that Sunday when you were six. You tugged on my sleeve during the invitation and told me you wanted to invite Jesus into your heart. I looked into those big blue eyes of yours and saw a new boy—a boy that has loved Jesus ever since. God will do great things through you. Bless you, child.

Susan, I have thanked God every day that you came into our family. When I told you that you were Adam's angel, I meant it. Before meeting you, Adam had something of a wild streak and dated some girls that Howard and I knew weren't right for him. Then you joined our church and suddenly Adam had a reason to be interested in church again. He may have started going for the wrong reason, but the right message got through. You are more than my daughter-in-law. You are also my daughter-in-Christ. I thank you for your devotion to Jesus and to my son. May God's love continue to shine through you.

Jim, since Melody was born, I have prayed for a good strong Christian husband for her. God answered my prayers in you. You have been an excellent husband and father, the big brother that Adam always wanted and needed, and a treasured son to us. I remember how proud I was when you were ordained as a deacon. You have the humble attitude of a servant that Jesus so beautifully demonstrated for us. Keep yourself immersed in the Bible and may God continue to reveal the truth of His Word to you as you serve Him by serving others.

Adam, I am so proud of the man you became. Though, through those turbulent teen years, your father and I spent many nights on our knees in prayer. God answers prayer—you are proof of that. From your rocky start at birth through the dangers you put yourself in as a teen, God protected you. Through it all we never stopped loving you or gave up on you—and neither did God. And, now here you are a youth minister, using your experiences and trials to help other troubled teens. God really does use everything for our good when we love Him and are called according to His purpose. May you continue to experience and show others that His mercies are new every morning.

Melody, my precious first-born, the day we brought you home from the hospital, your father and I just laid on the bed with you and marveled at how intricately and wonderfully you were made. Your first Christmas I made special stuffed animal decorations for the tree, so if you pulled the tree down, nothing would break. We still use many of those same ornaments. You have always been the worrier. But remember dear, God is in control, and nothing happens without His permission. I pass the torch to you now. You are the oldest woman in the family and I have taught you well. I know you miss me. The bond between mothers and daughters is so special. But you abide in Jesus and I am with Jesus, so I am truly in your heart as well. May God fill you with strength and wisdom.

Howard, as much as I love you, you have always known that someone else held first place in my heart—Jesus. And you would not have had it any other way because He held the same place in yours. And, because we put Jesus before each other, we shared a life and love that the world envies, but doesn't understand. Jesus isn't just part of our lives—He *is* our lives. And dear, when it's time for you to come home, I'll meet you at the gates. Until then, you continue to carry on the celebration of life with our family on earth and I will celebrate with our family here in heaven.

I ask all of you to continue to celebrate Christmas as I have taught you over the years, *(Howard's voice joins Marjorie's)* because it really wasn't me that made Christmas special. *(Marjorie exits)*

Howard: *(Continues reading)* It's Jesus that makes Christmas special. Christmas isn't just about the birth of a baby in a stable. It's about the blood sacrifice and victory over death too. You can't separate the manger, the cross, and the empty tomb any more than you can separate us from His love—or you from my love. So, my dear ones, get those decorations out, start the baking, and tell everyone you meet, Merry Christmas!

B.C. Tonight: Special Delivery

by Ammie Sullivent

Characters:
- Sandy Beach, news anchor
- Swift Current, news anchor
- Rain Forrest, weatherman
- Windy Gail, reporter
- Zechariah
- Elizabeth
- Storm Chaser, reporter
- King Herod
- Herod's two guards
- Harvest Moon, reporter
- Two Shepherds
- Rocky Hill, reporter
- Three Kings
- Smokey Stack, animal translator
- Rosey Bush, reporter
- Chicken
- Sheep
- Cow
- Crystal Waters, reporter
- Gabriel
- Rusty Nail, reporter
- Simeon
- Anna
- Joseph
- Mary with baby Jesus

Purpose: "BC Tonight: Special Delivery" emphasizes the fact that the birth of our Lord and Savior changed the world forever. The play highlights the main biblical figures of the event in the modern view of television news reporting. One can only imagine what it would have been like if Christ were born in our techno-driven age.

Production: Center stage is set as a news desk with microphones, coffee cups, and chairs for two anchors. Hanging from front of desk is sign that reads, "BC Tonight." The backdrops for the various scenes hang from stands on both sides of stage. This allows for scene changes without interruptions of play. The backdrops can be painted on white sheets or on paper or cardboard. Each reporter should be in business attire. The characters being interviewed are costumed accordingly.

Props: News desk (table with neutral, heavy, floor-length tablecloth), two chairs, two microphones for anchors, two coffee cups, sign, various backdrops for on-the-spot reporting, two microphones (one for each side of the stage, to be shared by on-the-spot reporters), feather, costumes for people being interviewed.

Length: 20-30 minutes

Scene 1:

Sandy Beach: Good Evening, I'm Sandy Beach . . .

Swift Current: . . . and I'm Swift Current

Both: Welcome to "B.C. Tonight—Special Delivery!!!"

Sandy: *(Very excited)* This is probably the most exciting show we have ever done.

Swift: *(Enthusiastically)* That's right Sandy; we are talking major change in the air. Tonight we'll be tracing the events of what some are saying may be the arrival of the Messiah.

Sandy: The events astonishingly resemble what the prophets foretold. Swift, we'll speak with everyone involved, but first to our local forecast. Over to you, Rain Forrest.

Rain Forrest: Thank you, Swift and Sandy. *(Looks up to sky and back at audience)* It looks like calm skies tonight. There is a spectacular show in the stars. If you go out, look to the east and you will see an amazingly bright star. *(Drops feather to check wind)* Winds are light with a slight breeze from the east. We are in for peaceful weather this joyful evening. Back to you, Sandy and Swift.

Sandy: Thank you; Rain. First up tonight we will visit the home of Zechariah and Elizabeth. Let's go to our correspondent, Windy Gail. Windy, can you hear me?

Windy: *(Holding pretend microphone and earpiece in ear)* I can hear you just fine. I'm here with Priest Zechariah and his wife Elizabeth. Tell me, Zechariah, about the amazing delivery you have received.

Zechariah: This started when I was at work in the temple. I had to go into a room and burn incense for the Lord. While I was in there an angel appeared to me and said Elizabeth and I would have a son. The angel said many would rejoice and that our son would be great in the sight of the Lord. This boy will pave the way for the Messiah.

Windy: Really, that is amazing. I mean obviously you are both up there in age! Who would have thought that you would be having a child now?

Zechariah: That's what I thought too!

Windy: How did you finally believe the angel?

Zechariah: I asked how I could be sure of this and the angel told me I would not be able to speak until it came to pass.

Elizabeth: Sure enough, I became pregnant. God showed me favor and kept His word.

Windy: Elizabeth, how was your pregnancy?

Elizabeth: It was fine! I was a little worried because of my age, but it really went well. My son even leaped for joy in my womb when my relative Mary came to visit. It was as if he knew she was going to give birth to the Messiah.

Windy: Zechariah, when did you get your voice back?

Zechariah: When Elizabeth told the priest we were naming our son John . . .

Elizabeth: *(Interrupting)* He didn't believe me. He didn't understand because John was not a family name.

Zechariah: I wrote on a tablet, "His name is John" and immediately I could speak.

Windy: How did that make everyone feel?

Zechariah: They knew just how special my boy was. They wondered what he was going to be because the Lord was with him. I praised the Lord!

Windy: That's great! Now back to the news desk. Sandy . . . Swift . . .

Swift: Thank you, Windy. What a story! If that wasn't enough, we now have an interview with the king himself, Herod the Great. We are off to the palace and our reporter, Storm Chaser.

Storm: *(Holding microphone and imaginary earpiece, bows to the king and then begins to speak)* Oh great King Herod, I can tell the news of this delivery troubles you and many others. Why is that?

King: The people are calling this wee one the King of the Jews. Huh, should a mere babe really threaten me?

Storm: Well, you seem so agitated. What are you going to do with this news? What if it is true and this child is the Messiah?

King: The Magi from the east will soon return to me and tell me where I can find this tot.

Storm: And then what will you do?

King: I cannot disclose the details, but an infant will not dethrone me!

Storm: What if by some chance the Magi betray you?

King: Then I will have to destroy all the boys who are two years old or younger.

Storm: Great King, that seems awfully harsh. Isn't there some other way?

King: *(To guards)* Take this man away. Lock him up! Throw him to the lions. Be rid of him and his questions. *(Guards pick Storm up by arms and carry him down the church aisle)*

Storm: *(In great distress)* Help me! Sandy! Swift! Anyone! Help! Help!

Sandy: *(Obviously baffled by what just happened)* Swift, do we send for him?

Swift: *(With cheesy grin)* He'll be fine. *(Moves finger across throat)* Let's go to our next interview with the shepherds who were watching their flocks by night. Over to you, Harvest Moon.

Harvest: *(Holding microphone and imaginary earpiece)* Thank you, Swift and Sandy. I'm here with a few of the shepherds. They say they actually saw the Christ-child. Tell me your story, fellas.

Shepherd #1: We were out there in that there field just a watchin' some sheep and an angel shows up.

Shepherd #2: *(Goofy, country accent)* "Angels From the Realms of Glory"

Shepherd #1: That was real pretty, but we was plumb scared.

Shepherd #2: "O Holy Night," we were scared!

Shepherd #1: The angel told us not to be afraid and that he was bringing good news of great joy for all people.

Shepherd #2: "Joy to the World!"

Shepherd #1: That angel told us where to find the Savior, Christ the Lord.

Shepherd #2: "Away in a Manger"

Harvest: So what did you do then?

Shepherd #1: We saw a great company of heavenly host and they praised God.

Shepherd #2: We said to each other, "Hark the Herald Angels Sing."

Shepherd #1: I said to the others, let's go to Bethlehem and see this thing that has happened.

Shepherd #2: Here we come, "O, Little Town of Bethlehem"

Shepherd #1: There we found Mary and Joseph. And there was the baby lying in a manger.

Shepherd #2: We shouted, "Go Tell It on the Mountain!"

Harvest: That's amazing, really amazing, back to you, Swift and Sandy.

Sandy: Thank you for that great story, Harvest. Swift, can you believe what we are hearing?

Swift: *(Skeptically)* I don't know Sandy. Let's go over to Rocky Hill who has located the Magi. Rocky, what do the Magi have to say about what they have seen?

Rocky: *(Holding microphone and imaginary earpiece)* Swift, Sandy . . . The Magi are also amazed by the events. Sirs, tell the people your story.

King 1: We saw the Star of the King of the Jews appear in the sky, so we came to find Him.

King 2: We asked King Herod where we might find this royal one, but he seemed rather angry.

King 3: He told us, according to the prophets, the King would be in Bethlehem.

King 1: He asked us when the star appeared and wants us to tell him where we found the child when we return.

King 2: We followed the star east until it stopped.

King 3: There we found the child. We were overjoyed.

King 1: We bowed down and worshiped Him.

Rocky: It's been said that you presented him some really nice gifts.

King 1: Yes, we did . . . Gold . . .

King 2: Incense . . .

King 3: and Myrrh . . .

Rocky: Wow, that was nice. So are you going back to King Herod?

King 1: No way! We were warned in a dream not to go back.

King 2: We'll go home a different way.

King 3: Hopefully King Herod's not watching.

Rocky: I think he might be busy taking care of a prisoner. Thank you for sharing your story. You must be on your way. Have a safe journey . . . Back to you at the news desk.

Swift: Great report, Rocky. Next we will go to the stable where this event supposedly took place.

Sandy: We will join Rosey Bush with the renowned animal psychologist and translator, Smokey Stack.

Rosey: (*Holding microphone and imaginary earpiece*) Thank you, Sandy and Swift. Smokey, I am so thrilled to be here with you today! I love it when you talk to the animals. Would you please ask the sheep to tell us what took place in their stable.

Smokey: *(To sheep)* Baa, baa baa baaaaa.

Sheep: Baa, baa, baa baa baa baa baa baa baa.

Smokey: *(To Rosey)* It seems a man and woman had a baby in here.

Rosey: Smokey, could you ask the cow why they would have a baby in the stable instead of the inn?

Smokey: Moo, moo moo moooooo.

Cow: Moo moo moooo moo moo.

Smokey: Rosey, the inn was completely full but the innkeeper offered them the shelter of this cozy stable.

Rosey: How did the animals feel about this event they witnessed?

Smokey: Moo moo, baa baa, cluck cluck.

Animals: *(All together make their sounds excitedly dancing with their arms in the air, flapping wings, etc.)*

Smokey: They were filled with great joy and wanted to celebrate.

Rosey: What happened after the birth of the child?

Smokey: *(To chicken)* Cluck cluck cluck clueeck.

Chicken: Cluck, cluck, cluueeckkk.

Smokey: The woman swaddled the babe in cloths and placed Him in the manger.

Rosey: Then what happened?

Smokey: *(To sheep)* baa baa baa baaaaa.

Sheep: Baa baa baa baaaa baaa ba baa baa ba ba ba ba ba.

Smokey: Some shepherds came in the stable; the animals were afraid they might bring in more sheep and disturb their peaceful, comfortable life, but the men bowed down and worshiped the baby.

Sheep: Baa baa ba ba ba.

Smokey: The sheep said He truly must be wonderful.

Rosey: Thank you, Smokey for your assistance. The world is a better place with you in it. Please thank the animals for sharing their story.

Smokey: *(To animals)* Baaa baaa, cluck cluck, moo moo.

Animals: *(All make their sound and wave good-bye)*

Rosey: That's it from the stable. Back to you, Swift and Sandy.

Swift: Every time Smokey is with us I really begin to understand animals so much better.

Sandy: They seem so excited. This story keeps getting better and better.

Swift: Now we are going to Crystal Waters.

Crystal: *(Holding microphone and imaginary earpiece)* Good Evening, Swift and Sandy. I'm here with a very exclusive interview. With me today is the angel who spoke to the young Mary and her soon-to-be husband Joseph. Gabriel, you claim to be a messenger of God. Is there any way to prove your claim?

Gabriel: I do not have to prove anything to anyone as long as I deliver the messages of my Master, the almighty God. I answer only to Him.

Crystal: You say you spoke to a young lady named Mary?

Gabriel: Yes, that is correct.

Crystal: What did you say to her?

Gabriel: I told her exactly what God told me to tell her.

Crystal: What was that?

Gabriel: That is confidential. Only God and Mary can tell you what was said.

Crystal: You also spoke to Joseph. What did you tell him? Did you explain how all this would come to pass?

Gabriel: I'm sorry but your line of questioning cannot be answered. Everything that went down with Joseph, Mary, Elizabeth, and Zechariah will be revealed in time. I must be going. The Great One has more for me to do. My greatest joy is serving my God. *(Walks off stage)*

Crystal: *(Discouraged and frustrated)* Swift, Sandy, that's all from me.

Sandy: It looks like God has full control of that one. Swift, where are we off to now?

Swift: Sandy, we are now going to our temple reporter, Rusty Nail. Rusty, who do you have with you?

Rusty: *(Holding microphone and imaginary earpiece)* I have with me a gentleman by the name of Simeon and a sweet lady named Anna. Anna, let's start with you . . . Ladies first as they say . . . What happened here that makes you believe the Messiah has come?

Anna: I am a prophetess and I have been in the temple many years. I worship night and day. I fast and I pray. That's how I knew when I saw that precious baby that He was the Son of God.

Rusty: So when you saw the child what did you do?

Anna: I gave thanks to God.

Rusty: Wow, Anna, you really did see the Messiah!

Anna: *(With passion)* I'm going to tell all who have been looking forward to the redemption of Jerusalem.

Rusty: Simeon, I've heard you are a very righteous and devout person. Why are you in the temple all the time?

Simeon: I have been waiting on the consolation of Israel. The Holy Spirit told me I would live until I saw the Lord's Christ.

Rusty: So tell me, Simeon, what you experienced.

Simeon: The parents brought Him into the temple to present Him to the Lord. The Law requires every firstborn male to be consecrated to the Lord. I took the child in my arms and I praised God.

Rusty: What did you say to God?

Simeon: I told God I could peacefully pass on because I have seen salvation.

Rusty: How can you be sure?

Simeon: The Holy Spirit is upon me and I trust in God completely.

Rusty: Did you speak to the parents?

Simeon: Yes, I blessed them and said to Mary, His mother, that this child is destined to cause the falling and rising of many in Israel, and a sign that will be spoken against, so that the thoughts of many hearts will be revealed. And a sword will pierce her soul too.

Rusty: Thank you so much, Anna and Simeon. You are truly a blessing. Back to the studio.

Swift: *(Getting slightly emotional)* What a story! Sandy, it is time for our very special guests. Welcome to the studio, Joseph, Mary, and their son, Jesus.

Sandy: We are so excited to have you with us. Mary; we talked to the angel Gabriel, but he didn't give us much information. What did Gabriel say to you?

Mary: He referred to me as highly favored and told me the Lord was with me.

Sandy: Why do you think you are considered highly favored?

Mary: *(Shyly)* I don't know exactly. I am obedient to the Lord and trust Him fully with my life. I am humbled to be His servant.

Sandy: What else did Gabriel say?

Mary: He told me I would be with child and have a son. He said I was to name Him Jesus.

Sandy: Did you believe what you heard?

Mary: I believed, I mean Gabriel was a messenger from God, but I questioned how this could be. *(Shyly adding)* I mean, . . . we weren't even married yet.

Sandy: How did he answer?

Mary: He told me the Holy Spirit would be upon me and the power of the Most High would overshadow me, that the one to be born would be called the Son of God.

Sandy: So did it all come to pass like it was foretold?

Mary: Exactly as it was said, it happened.

Swift: Joseph, I have to say, I am surprised you went through with your wedding to Mary. I mean finding out she was with child and all. What kept you from turning her out?

Joseph: An angel appeared to me in a dream and told me what was going on. The angel also told me to name the baby Jesus. So when I awoke I did as I was told.

Swift: What took you to Bethlehem?

Joseph: Caesar Augustus issued a decree that a census should be taken. I had to take my wife to register in my family's homeland, the City of David.

Sandy: Mary, was that a difficult journey for you?

Mary: I was great with child. It was pretty rough. Then there weren't any available rooms at the inn. At least the stable was some shelter.

Swift: What went through your mind when shepherds began to worship your newborn Son?

Mary: I treasured those things and pondered them in my heart.

Joseph: We knew how special this delivery really was.

Swift: And the gifts from the Magi?

Mary: *(Lovingly)* The gold, incense, and myrrh.

Joseph: All the gifts have special meaning. I would like to thank the Magi for not giving in to the pressure of King Herod.

Sandy: And the blessings at the temple?

Mary: It all confirms what the angel said. This baby is the Son of God, Jesus the Christ.

Swift: Sandy, I have just been handed a note from our producer. It seems due to the overwhelming evidence of the truth, our show will be renamed A.D. Today!

Sandy: What does A.D. mean?

Swift: It is short for *Anno Domini*, which means the Year of our Lord.

Sandy: That's wonderful. I am so excited about these events. It should really change the world.

Swift: That wraps up this report of a very special delivery.

Sandy and Swift: Join us in the morning for "A.D. Today."

Christmas Traditions

by Mary Martin

Characters: -Katie, volunteer at the mission, has a heart for children
-Theresa, director of children's Christmas program at church
-Amy, Theresa's assistant
-Mandy, Katie's friend
-Children: Small group at the mission, larger group at the church
-Child 1 (church)
-Child 2 (church)
-Child 3 (church)
-Child 4 (church)
-Stevie (church)
-Jessica (church)
-Luke (mission)
-Tina (mission)

Purpose: Jesus was born into our world as a helpless infant—nothing regal, nothing spectacular. When He left our world, He asked us to do one thing: to love others into a relationship with Christ. Today we find ourselves pulled in a multitude of directions within a society that wants bigger, louder, faster—from everything. In "Christmas Traditions," Theresa and Amy are struggling to get the annual children's Christmas presentation together. Theresa desperately wants something new and fresh and believes that Katie is the perfect creative person for the job. Katie, however, is too busy shopping to help. Theresa struggles with anger and frustration toward Katie, until she finds out that Katie was shopping for children at the local mission.

For more dramas from this author visit www.ihgproductions.com

After the two have an in-depth discussion, Theresa discovers that Katie has been investing more than just money in the children. Some Christmas traditions cannot be presented on a stage and are only effective when demonstrated in the lives of people who may never enter a church building.

Production: Alternate scenes between a church where Theresa, Amy, and the church children are practicing a Christmas program and a local mission where Katie and Mandy meet with the mission children. Scene 3 takes place at the church and the mission simultaneously.

- Suggested Songs: Throughout the script the church children are rehearsing their songs. We have included traditional song title suggestions *(in italics)*, however these can easily be substituted and should reflect songs that your children's choir/ensemble can perform and yet fit within the framework of the story.

- Musician(s): While there is not a specific character written into this script (although Theresa or Amy could serve as the accompanist), ensembles that sing with live accompaniment will need to adjust accordingly; e.g., piano/keyboard player; ensembles singing with tape/CD should have an audio person who is familiar with the script.

Props:

- Church Scene: This should look like an affluent church that is in the middle of producing a Christmas program—possible props may include risers, children's nativity costumes, unfinished scenery that is in disarray around the stage, floor microphone, music stand, music instruments as desired. Theresa must have coffee!

- Mission: In stark contrast to the church—possible props may include a few worn chairs, a scraggly Christmas tree with an old blanket or towel as a skirt, gifts in used plastic bags wrapped with brown paper. Katie should have Hershey's Kisses and some other candy on hand.

- Clothing: Theresa is richly dressed for the holiday season, while Katie dresses in a manner that is plain and understated. The church children should be well dressed, while the mission children should look underprivileged.

Length: 20-25 minutes (without music)

Scene 1:

The Church

Child 1:	Look! It's Katie!
Child 2:	Hey Katie! Do you have any peppermints left?
Child 3:	How about cinnamons?
Katie:	Sure. In this pocket.
Child 4:	You're awesome! Thanks!
Child 2:	Yeah, thanks Katie. You rock!
Katie:	No problem. *(Notices little shy boy sort of lost in shuffle of kids)* Hey Stevie, how about a kiss?
Stevie:	No way!
Katie:	Okay then, I'll just have to eat it myself. *(Pulls out a chocolate kiss)*
Stevie:	Wait! *(Katie pops the chocolate kiss in her mouth)* You don't have another one do you?
Katie:	Why? Change your mind? Lucky for you I've got a backup kiss. *(Flips a candy kiss to him)*
Stevie:	Thanks, Katie. *(Turns to go, then turns back to Katie)* You're the best.
Katie:	Nope! Chocolate is the best! *(Winks)*
Theresa:	*(Claps hands)* All right kids, let's go! We've got a lot of work to do.
Katie:	You guys better get cracking! *(Kids leave Katie—some hug her—and head over to risers)* Hey, break a leg!
Theresa:	How about a hand with rehearsal, Katie?
Katie:	Sorry, Theresa. I can't. My ride is here.

Enter Mandy.

Mandy:	Hey Katie! Ready? Only twelve days 'til Christmas. We've got to hustle, girl!

Katie:	Christmas hustle! The new dance craze that's sweeping the nation! Goes like this! *(Dances off with Mandy laughing)*
Theresa:	*(To Amy)* Must be nice to waltz away from work and responsibility.
Amy:	*(Laughs)* Katie's lively all right, but she works hard at a lot of things.
Theresa:	Passing out free candy and flitting off on a shopping spree hardly qualifies as hard work.
Amy:	You obviously haven't tackled the mob at the mall lately!
Theresa:	Never mind. *We* have work to do. *(Claps hands and says to children)* All right. Everyone in your places please. Let's start with "Hark! The Herald Angels Sing."

Suggested Song: "Hark! The Herald Angels Sing"

Children sing.

Theresa:	*(Immediately at end of song)* Marvelous. Next, break into your practice groups and read through your lines. *(Children leave risers and settle into groups)* Quietly please. *(To Amy)* You know, *this* is when we could use extra help. I've asked Katie several times, but she always has an excuse—lately it seems there's always a previous shopping engagement.
Amy:	Katie *does* shop a lot. She loves to give gifts.
Theresa:	Must be nice. But, honestly, a little of her *precious* time would be a far better gift. *(Amy looks disapprovingly)* I know. That was snide. It's just that there's so much work to do. And we could use the extra help. Katie would be perfect. She has a great rapport with the kids. They all love her.
Amy:	No doubt the kids love her. And she would be a huge help. But she's not slacking. She just chooses to celebrate Christmas differently.
Theresa:	Oh, less church, more shopping?
Amy:	Theresa! Katie has her reasons. *(Lights fade to black)*

Scene 2:

The Mission (before children arrive)

Katie:	*(Entering with Mandy; both are carrying bags filled with brown paper wrapped packages)* Are these great deals or what!

Mandy: Totally! It was awesome!

Katie: I picked up the necessities. *And* a few extras. (*Pulls out small book-shaped package*) It's a journal for private thoughts. Tina will absolutely love the cover!

Mandy: Tina absolutely loves *you*. All the kids do.

Katie: I love them too. Now look at this. Do you think this devotional is right for Luke?

Mandy: It's perfect. All the gifts are. I'm amazed how you fit the gift to each child.

Katie: I think I just found all the right sales!

Mandy: *And* I'm amazed at how you deflect compliments with such finesse! You are way awesome, Katie. Do you know that? Do you get how much you mean to these kids?

Katie: I'm not all that. Really.

Mandy: You are! How many people would do what you do?

Katie: Lots of people would. Really. It's no big deal.

Mandy: I don't see lots of people volunteering, Katie. At least not year-round like you do. Sure, anyone can write a check or do the holiday guilt trip thing. But to Tina, to Luke, and to all the others, well, what you do *is* a big deal!

Katie: *God* is the big deal, Mandy. He gives me more than I need. All I do is share what He gives. God keeps giving and I keep sharing. It's as simple as that.

Mandy: Well, God sure gives to the right person. Not everyone shares as freely as you do.

Katie: I have all I need. Those kids don't. How can I hold on to extra when they don't even have the necessities?

Mandy: Whatever! Blow it off all you want. But, like I said, *you* are totally awesome.

Katie: Mandy! (*Throws something soft at her*)

Mandy: Okay. God is totally awesome too! (*Lights fade to black*)

Scene 3:

The Church and the Mission

Theresa: *(Claps hands)* All right everyone, let's run that again. Jessica, say your lines a little louder and a lot slower.

Jessica: *(Reciting into mic the traditional Christmas story in a very rehearsed fashion)* Behold, I bring you good tidings of great joy, which shall be to all people. For unto you is born this day in the city of David, a Savior, which is Christ, the Lord. And this shall be a sign unto you. You shall find the babe wrapped in swaddling clothes and lying in a manger. *(Add more as desired)*

Theresa: Well done, Jessica. Choir? *(Motions them to sing)*

Suggested Song: "Away in a Manger"

Children sing.

Theresa: The singing was fantastic, but the boys in the back need to keep their hands to themselves please. And no more toe-tapping on the risers. It's very distracting. Amy? Do we have Mary and Joseph ready yet?

Amy: Ready!

Theresa: All right choir. Let's hear "O Come, All Ye Faithful".

Suggested Song: "O Come, all Ye Faithful"

As children sing, Mary and Joseph slowly and reverently enter. After a few moments, the wise men begin to walk onstage unsure of themselves.

Theresa: *(Loudly, over the singing)* No! No! No! *(Singing stops)* No wise men! Not yet! All right everyone. Let's take a fifteen-minute break! Amy, would you *please* bring me a cup of coffee?

Amy: Already poured it.

Theresa: You're a gem. *(Drinks coffee and sighs heavily)* I'd rather be shopping. *(Pause)* Now explain to me again why shopping isn't slacking.

Amy: Back to Katie, huh? That's really eating you up isn't it?

Theresa: I hate to admit it.

Amy: Admitting your dysfunction is the first step toward recovery.

Theresa: All right, wise guy.

Amy: Hey! I thought you said it wasn't time for the wise guys! *(Laughs while Theresa glares)* All right! All right! I was just kidding.

Theresa: Now give me a reason why I shouldn't choke both you and Katie?

Amy: Me? Because I make the best cup of coffee in town.

Theresa: True. Thanks.

Amy: Katie? Because she's awesome with kids.

Theresa: I know that! That's why I need her here! *(To children)* All right everyone, in your places. Let's pick it up where we left off.

Suggested Song: "Silent Night, Holy Night"

(Children begin singing "Silent Night." After first verse, ensemble should sing quietly while Katie begins telling the Christmas story to the mission children with great excitement and animation. Lights should fade out over choir and come up over Katie and the children. If ensemble is too loud, singers may drop out.)

Katie: It all started many years ago, in sheep country. The shepherds there were keeping a sharp eye out for wolves and lions and other sheep-eating animals that prowl around at night looking to snatch up a tasty to-go snack. When all of a sudden, the night sky burst open. Beams of light were shooting in every direction and angels were popping out all over, singing Glory Hallelujahs and all sorts of heavenly songs. Well, those shepherds had never seen angels before. And just the sight of such heavenly beings got the poor fellows trembling and shaking so that their very teeth rattled and chattered in their heads. Their knees were knocking so hard they could barely stand at all. As a matter of fact, those rugged shepherds were so scared their legs became as jiggly as gelatin. Of course, everyone knows that you can't stand on legs that are acting like Jello Jigglers, so those poor petrified shepherds fell flat out on their faces in fright. And you know what the angels did then?

Tina: Did they sing some more?

Katie: Well, they wanted to. That's for sure. Angels love singing Glory Hallelujahs and such, but they couldn't just break out in a round of "O Come, All Ye Faithful" and leave those poor, trembling shepherds on their faces. So, one of them spoke up and said "Hey! Don't be afraid. I have great news! This message is for you, for your neighbors, for everyone, everywhere! Listen now! A child has just been born in David's town. He is the Savior! He is the Christ! He is the King! And this is how you will recognize Him. Look for a baby boy all wrapped up and lying in a manger." And once the angel said that, well all the other angels began to sing again. This time they sang a great many glories to God and even a peace to all on earth.

Luke: After that, the shepherds went to look for the baby, huh?

Katie: That's exactly what they did. Those shepherds jumped up, brushed off, and scurried away to David's town as fast as their sandals would carry them.

Luke: David's town is Bethlehem, right Katie?

Katie: Yep! And those shepherds couldn't get to Bethlehem fast enough. But when they arrived, they stopped dead in their tracks. They were awestruck. For there, in the manger, right before their eyes, just as the angels had said, was the little baby. Well, what do you think those shepherds did then?

Tina: What *did* they do, Katie?

Katie: Well, those shepherds did what anyone would do. They ran around telling everyone. They told everyone they knew. They told everyone they met. They told every last detail—from the angels in the countryside to the baby in the manger. And everyone who heard the story thought it was totally awesome! Pretty exciting for a small town in Bible times. But what about now, in our times, in our town? How is the birth of the baby, King Jesus, important to us today? That's what I want you to think about for the next time.

Luke: Awww. Come on Katie. You're not leaving are you?

Tina: Aren't you going to tell us what happens next?

Katie: Consider it a cliffhanger. Here's another one . . . why would Jesus even think about leaving His home in heaven just to be born in a smelly old barn? Wrestle with that one a while and we'll talk again next time.

Lights fade over Katie and the mission children and come up over Theresa and the church children.

Theresa: All right. Last time through on "We Wish You a Merry Christmas."

Suggested Song: "We Wish You a Merry Christmas"

Children sing.

Theresa: *(Immediately when song is finished)* Much better. Good job everyone. Don't forget to practice with your tapes. Every day. Those of you with lines, please work on memorization. I'll see you all next Wednesday at six.

Amy: So, other than the usual rowdies in the back row, practice went well.

Theresa: Yeah. It wasn't bad. But it needs something.

Amy: What?

Theresa: Pizzazz—panache—something new, something fresh. I don't know. That's another reason why I wanted Katie to help. She's full of pizzazz.

Amy: I know where you can find her.

Theresa: Where?

Amy: At the Seventh Street Mission. She volunteers with the children there.

Theresa: Really?

Amy: Really. She loves those kids. She tells them stories, plays games, and listens to all their jokes and riddles, over and over again. And she laughs every time.

Theresa: So, all the shopping . . . is for the mission kids?

Katie: *(Entering quickly)* Busted!

Theresa: Katie? *(Frustrated)* You're too late. Rehearsal is over.

Katie: I know. I saw the kids leaving. Besides, I didn't come to help with rehearsal.

Theresa: Well, what *did* you come for?

Katie: I came to talk to you.

Theresa: About why you keep sneaking off just when rehearsal is about to start?

Katie: I thought it might look that way. So I came to straighten things out.

Theresa: So you *will* help?

Katie: No. I made a commitment to the kids at the Seventh Street Mission. But there are plenty of people who've been part of the church much longer than I have. They could help. They know the whole Christmas program routine. Besides, I'm not really all that traditional when it comes to Christmas.

Amy: *(Hurriedly)* I'll get the coffee. *(Exits)*

Theresa: Tradition is an important element in celebrating Christmas.

Katie: Don't get me wrong. Some traditions are great. I have a few myself.

Theresa: But?

Katie: But, *some* traditions actually shove Christ out of the spotlight. When that happens, families—even entire churches—squabble, sometimes ferociously, with one another. You've seen it. People brawling over music, styles of worship, and even choir robes! In the meantime, Jesus is lost in the scuffle. Pretty pathetic when you consider that Christmas is one time of the year when Christians can openly and vividly convey the message of Christ. As a matter of fact, speaking as a former non-Christian, the world expects it and is cynically disappointed when Christians fail so miserably.

Amy: *(Entering, hands coffee to Theresa)* How's that?

Katie: Well, think of it this way. How can anyone *outside* the church buy into the message of Christ when those *inside* the church don't?

Theresa: Wait a minute! What are you trying to say?

Katie: I'm just saying that the message of Christ is skewed not only by what we say, but also by what we do—or don't do for that matter. If Jesus is really the "reason for the season" then why does He get so little of the focus?

Theresa: Is that the way you see it?

Katie: That's the way a lot of people outside the church see it. So they cynically condemn what they see as sanctimonious self-entertainment and ironically, they walk away disappointed. They *expect* Christians to be over-the-top with Jesus—especially during Christmas. They understand sacrifice, commitment, and investment in principles. And they're watching to see if the church is for real—or just another scam.

Amy: So what's your idea of an over-the-top Christmas?

Katie: Well, look at the shepherds in the Christmas story. They were pretty over-the-top! And their message was pretty over-the-top too. I mean angels bursting out of the sky and a baby king born in a barn to be a savior to everyone? But they took a risk. They told everyone! And what enthusiasm they had—because they believed it themselves—they were fueled by faith in an amazing promise of hope.

Theresa: So what you're saying is, the church needs more enthusiasm?

Katie: Well, I *have* seen more zealots for the latest cappuccino flavor than for Jesus lately, but that's not all the church needs.

Amy: What else then? Faith?

Katie: Yes, faith and enthusiasm, but also vision. Unfortunately, the church has forgotten its purpose. Rather than spreading the news and multiplying ourselves, we spend most of our time inside a building with people who are already in on God's rescue plan.

Theresa: I've been so busy with this Christmas Eve service.

Katie: That's precisely my point! We're so busy *doing* church that we have no time to do what our Father asked us to do. So, even though we look like we're doing the right thing, we wind up doing it all wrong. It's not that what we're doing is necessarily sinful. It's just not what we were asked to do.

Amy: This reminds me of Paul's do and don't do message in Romans.

Katie: It does get pretty tricky. Think of it this way. What if the kids in the Christmas Eve service practiced *painting* instead of *singing.* What if they painted all the Sunday school rooms? Maybe they created vibrant murals down the walls of the main hallway—all portraying biblical characters? Nothing sinful about that. As a matter of fact, it's shows talent, ability, commitment, and creativity. But they're still disobedient. Why? Because they didn't do what they were asked to do. They got sidetracked. They failed to complete the task they were given. It's the same with us! We've gotten sidetracked, investing our talents and abilities in all sorts of creative ways. In the end, we wind up being disobedient children. Meanwhile, our heavenly Father is waiting for us to remember who we are in Christ and what our purpose is.

Amy: So, what *is* our purpose?

Katie: Simple. One task. That's all He left us with. Just one. He asked us to love with reckless abandon—unconditionally. This is the way new Christ-followers are made. We are to love in such a way that we multiply ourselves and increase the family of God. Every program, every meeting, every worship service is more than an arm of ministry for the people of the church. It is an opportunity to love people into the family.

Amy: It's pretty clear when you say it that way. But you're talking about changing *years* of tradition.

Theresa: How do you turn a whole church around when it's charging off in the opposite direction?

Katie: It's too overwhelming when you look at the church as this massive organization. This is how I see it. The church isn't some nebulous entity out there I can point the finger of blame on. The church is *people*. That's me. And you. *We* are the church.

Amy: So what do *we*, the church, do?

Katie: We spend time with God. Talk with Him. Read His book. Do what He says. When in doubt, follow Jesus. No more, no less. Wholeheartedly.

Amy: It sounds simple, but radical.

Katie: That's the way it all began, with one simple but radical act of love—from the manger to the cross.

Savior Alone

by Blair and Mary Martin

Characters: -Brian, a pastor
-Keith, Brian's friend
-Alisha, an abused girl, age 14-18
-Jeremy, a young man whose mother has died
-Christine, Keith's sister

Purpose: "Savior Alone" is a drama series written specifically for the Advent season (the four weeks prior to Christmas). Although divided into four parts, it may also be presented within one service. The title of this drama—"Savior Alone"—has a double meaning, and the players should keep both in mind throughout the presentation.

First, it is the Savior alone, only Jesus Christ, who through His death and resurrection redeems us from our sins and gives us eternal life.

Second, when Jesus entered our world, He abdicated His position in heaven, left His Father God and took on the vulnerability of humanity—was subjected to the same physical limitations—by His own choosing. And when Jesus was nailed to the cross, because of His willingness to embrace and accept all our sin (on our behalf), He became separated from God. He was the Savior, alone in the manger, alone among people who did not understand Him, alone in prayer, and finally, alone on the cross—an ultimate sacrifice He made so we could overcome death.

For more dramas from these authors visit www.ihgproductions.com

Production: The themes within this drama represent the birth, life, and death of Jesus Christ and the hope He brings to the world. That hope is not for the world as a whole, but rather for the souls of the world—and He changes one soul at a time. The drama is divided in the following way:

- Part One: "One Soul at a Time." There is longing and despair in our world. We are all vulnerable, but Jesus understands vulnerability. He experienced it by coming to earth as an infant.

- Part Two: "Eye to Eye." There is a need for a rescuer. Jesus walked and lived among humans to show us He could build relationships. He had to reach out, to touch, and to offer His grace before anyone could understand it.

- Part Three: "Beyond Understanding." We need to be understood. And God does that. Emmanuel—God with us—the Savior who died on the cross, not so He could understand death, but so He could experience it. That is true understanding—Jesus with us through all our suffering.

- Part Four: "For Eternity." We are designed to belong. When Jesus overcame death, He restored our broken relationship with God. Once again we can fully belong with God because Jesus took sin, death, and Hell upon Himself.

The characters in "Savior Alone" are meant to connect with the audience rather than with each other. The actors should never interact on stage. Rather, they should speak at all times directly to the audience. This presentation style creates an ethereal quality to the drama and compels the audience to engage with each character as he or she speaks.

Songs: We recommend selecting appropriate titles that will best fit your church's ministry style. Throughout the script we have suggested places where music/congregational songs would be appropriate.

Suggested Visuals: Visuals are suggested for those churches that have media capabilities and would like to augment the script's impact. Many of the suggested images are symbolic of something deeper while others are less subtle. While the drama can stand alone without either songs or visuals, it is our purpose to provide a presentation that will cognitively and aesthetically engage, challenge, and impact those who experience it.

Props: "Savior Alone" was written with a minimum of props in mind. The idea is to focus on the characters rather than the stage setting. In addition, it is simple to present in even the smallest of churches. The only necessary items required are two cell phones and a chair. Each drama team may choose to add props as is appropriate for the setting or for personal taste.

Length: The times indicated below are approximations and do not include any music. Other factors to consider include delivery style, dramatic pauses, as well as the addition of physical movement or props.
-Part One: 5 minutes
-Part Two: 5 minutes
-Part Three: 6 minutes
-Part Four: 8 minutes
Total Length: 24 minutes

Part One:

"One Soul at a Time"

Setting: Brian enters on one side of the stage and addresses the audience throughout. Keith remains on the other side of the stage, seated in a chair, but he addresses Brian as if Brian is talking directly with him.

Brian: *(Entering to side of stage and speaking directly to audience)* I've been in ministry a long time. The last ten years as pastor right here. I thought it would get easier as the years passed, but that's just not true. *(Pause)* I think maybe it's the realization that as I grow older, I find that I know much less than I thought. I've spent too much of my life trying to mold God into something that I can contain—even manipulate. God is a great and magnificent mystery, and I'm just beginning to see more of that mystery in our lives—but it's something that I can't explain. *(Long pause)*

For example, what exactly is Advent? *(Pause)* I'm not talking about a definition; any of us can look that up. But it's also more than four colored candles and a countdown calendar. God meets us here. *(Points to heart)* I believe that without reservation—but how does that happen on a daily basis?

Keith: *(Sitting in a chair on the opposite side of the stage talking on a cell phone)* Look Brian, I don't really want to talk about this on the phone.

[Suggested Visuals: Through the following dialogue, present four to six pictures of a sky that sequentially darkens as storm clouds gather.]

Brian: Keith and I went to seminary together. I finished, but he never did. Don't get me wrong. He's a good man. And for quite a while he was a leader in his church. Many times when I needed a sympathetic ear, he was a great support for me—and I've tried to do the same for him. Over the last several years though, he's grown away from the church, maybe even from God. He called me the other day.

Keith: Nothing's going on this afternoon. Can you come by?

Brian: I told him I'd be there.

Keith: Thanks, Brian. *(Hangs up cell phone)*

Brian: I didn't know what to expect from Keith. I could tell something was bothering him. When I got to his home, he just sat there for a while, not saying anything, and then he leaned forward *(Keith leans forward)* and said *(Keith speaks line with Brian)* "I don't think I can do this anymore."

[Suggested Visuals: Dark sky with thunderclouds and lightning.]

Keith: It's not like it used to be. I was always with people, praying for them. Praying with them—offering them comfort when they were sick, when they were hurt, even when they were about to die. And they would accept that comfort. It's not the same now. Something's changed.

Brian: That's when I knew that Keith was touching on what I had been feeling.

[Suggested Visuals: City streets, dark and rainy, then pictures of human tragedies (e.g., 9/11, Iraq war, Sudanese conflict, etc.).]

Keith: People want to know that God is here. Not out there somewhere *(Waves his hand)* but right here. *(Forcefully)* Right here with us. But there's so much fear now—and no easy answer. The threat of war, the 9/11 tragedy, unprecedented levels of human depravity, and evil . . . How do I explain that God is here with us through all of that? I'm not even sure I can believe that He is.

Brian: He was right about one thing. There is no easy answer—we each experience pain uniquely. I think people today want a Mr. Fix-it for a God, some kind of celestial Santa Claus that dispenses blessings like a vending machine spits out candy.

[Suggested Visuals: Close-up of a face that expresses fear and/or vulnerability.]

Keith: The world is a frightening place.

Brian: I had to admit—at times I'm scared too.

Keith: We're all so vulnerable.

Brian: Here is the only thing I could think to say. In the flesh, yes, that's true—we are very vulnerable. But God knows that. And He doesn't know that just from understanding it. He knows about being vulnerable because He experienced it.

Keith: As a baby?

[Suggested Visuals: Newborn baby being held in masculine arms (or hands) suggesting the disparity between strength and weakness.]

Brian: What can be more helpless than a newborn?

Keith: So how do I work with that—where do I fit in?

Brian: *(Shaking his head)* I didn't have a pat answer. I'm sure Keith didn't want one. He needed something real to hold on to. I needed time to think. *(Visuals fade)*

Song(s)

Brian: Then some words from Isaiah 64 came into my head. I couldn't remember it completely—just the part that says: "Since ancient times no one has heard, no eye has seen any God besides you, who acts on behalf of those who wait for Him." (*Pause*)

Keith: (*Speaking slowly*) Our God who acts . . .

[Suggested Visuals: Earth as seen from space.]

Brian: . . . who came as an infant . . .

Keith: . . . who invaded our world . . .

Brian: . . . a world of unspeakable evil . . .

Keith: . . . to be with us.

Brian: That may be why God puts us where He does.

Keith: But I've never seen such despair—such longing in people.

Brian: I told him there was hope in despair.

Keith: I don't understand that.

Brian: I knew this was difficult to explain. I told him that in great times of desolation, we all grasp for whatever will help us from one moment to the next.

Keith: So, where is the hope?

Brian: You see, it's not hope in the world. It's hope for one soul—one soul at a time. That's who God is reaching out to. That's who He wants us to reach out to . . .

Keith: One soul . . .

Brian: . . . at a time.

Keith: (*Slowly*) One at a time—that's something I can still do.

Brian: Looking back on our conversation, I realize I didn't answer all his questions—how could I? (*Pause*) I thought we were finished, but then Keith said something else that brought it all home. Right where I live.

Keith: I need to tell you about some of those souls . . . some of those souls right here and now. *(Visuals and lights fade to black)*

Song(s)

Part Two:

"Eye To Eye"

Setting: Brian is on one side of the stage addressing the audience while Keith is on the other side. Keith is still in his chair.

Song(s)

Brian: *(Omit all dialogue up to Visuals on next page if presented within the same service; begin with Setting)* My friend, Keith, asked me to come to his house to talk to him. I'd known Keith for a long time—knew he just needed someone to listen to him. At one time, God had been such a vital part of his life, but over the years He had become less significant to Keith. As I listened, I began to hear Keith's heart. I began to empathize with how he had gotten to where he was today.

He told me about himself—about his feelings of vulnerability and how scared he felt to have to live in this world. I told him Jesus was born into our world as a vulnerable infant. I told him that because Jesus knows vulnerability, we have hope.

Honestly, I had come to see Keith not because I thought I could offer advice, but because I thought he needed someone to really hear his heart. And then when I heard Keith say there were souls he wanted to tell me about, I knew that listening might be all I could offer. *(Setting: Brian slowly exits and Alisha enters in his place as Keith delivers his lines)*

[Suggested Visuals: Throughout the following dialogue and until the song, there should be shots of a bustling city—buildings, automobiles, and people. The last shot should be of a young girl's face, preferably one who looks as if she has had a difficult life (it does not need to be the person playing Alisha—the visual is merely a representation of all the girls who have had similar circumstances).]

Keith: I met someone the other day. Her name was Alisha. You should have seen her. *(Pauses and then stands and addresses the audience as Brian had been)* Now I know things go on—things happen to people that no one should ever have to experience, but somehow I've always been insulated from all of that. I don't know if it's been good fortune or just the roll of the dice, but when you don't see that stuff with your own eyes, when you don't look eye to eye with someone who's in the middle of something, it's easy to forget that there's a world other than the one you've created around you. *(Long pause)* It was a fluke that we met. Maybe I was just in the wrong place at the wrong time—I don't know—but this girl—she needed someone to hear her. I'm sure what she said was only the tip of the iceberg, but it was enough.

Alisha: He looked at me and saw me. I wasn't just a piece of street trash that someone had kicked aside. *(Pause)* You can't understand that—not if you haven't lived every day like you're an object. Like you're either a bag of pleasure parts—some pervert's eye candy, or a damaged dime-store toy—used up and tossed to the curb with yesterday's garbage, or worse yet, a mist, a vapor—you know—see through—invisible. When you're invisible, you're no longer human. You're nothing. *(Long pause)* Of course, when you're invisible, when you're nothing, no one can get to you. No one can touch you. No one can hurt you. So, I practice being invisible. It's safer that way.

Keith: I found a stray dog one time. I put some food out for it, but it would never get close to me. It had wounds that needed tending—but it was too scared of me—or anyone—to allow someone to touch it.

Alisha: One time, I thought I was being invisible. I thought I'd made it past the drunk that was sprawled out on the living room couch—this one, my mother claimed, was my real father. I wasn't invisible enough. He slurred my name and staggered toward me. Stumbling, nearly falling, he was all over me—slobbering. I closed my eyes. *(Closes her eyes—long pause)* If I could just be invisible—if I could just be someone else—someone normal—with a normal life. If I could just have one normal day. *(Alisha exits as Keith speaks. Brian takes her place.)*

Keith: I didn't need to hear more. I was there for only a moment—just a fraction of her fractured life. Was it God who put me there to make a difference for Alisha? How could that be? And what was there to say? How could I touch her?

Song(s)

Brian: I had told Keith that people wanted a Santa Claus God—a Mr. Fix-it.

Keith: That's not what Alisha needed.

Brian: No—she needed a rescuer. Saying that she was looking for a Santa Claus God would be trite, dismissive.

Keith: I can't go to sleep at night without hearing her voice. Wondering what I can do so she can have just one normal day.

Brian: Jesus came to us as an infant, but He didn't stay an infant. He became empowered so He could accomplish great things.

Keith: But how?

Brian: I asked Keith if he kept putting food out for that dog.

Keith: Yes, but I don't know what happened to it.

[Suggested Visuals: Picture of inner city mission with people walking by, or several shots of homeless people, lying on the street or existing in makeshift shelters.]

Brian: Perhaps—ultimately—it's not what happened to it that counts. I told him he couldn't make the dog accept the food. What matters is that he offered.

Keith: Alisha is so demolished she can't even anticipate a rescue.

Brian: It's about risk—the risk it takes to keep offering, and then to act when the offer is accepted. Who knows how long it might be until someone is willing to take that first step—to reach for the outstretched hand. It's the first morsel of food that will move the dog from certain death to possible life.

Keith: *(Slowly)* To act—to live among others—to see someone invisible—to risk the offer.

Brian: That's what Jesus did. It's hope again—but still one soul at a time.

Keith: Let me tell you about another . . . *(Lights fade to black)*

Song(s):

Part Three:

"Beyond Understanding"

Setting: Both Keith and Brian are standing, facing the audience. They are on opposite ends of the stage from each other.

Song(s):

Brian: *(Omit until Setting on next page if presented within one service)* My friend, Keith, asked me to come to his house to talk to him. I'd known him for years, watched his fire for God slowly fade away. But during our conversation, I began to understand what he had been feeling, how he had lost his zeal. He told me about how he had been feeling vulnerable and scared in the world. I told him Jesus was born into our world as a vulnerable infant. Because Jesus knows vulnerability, we have hope. Keith also told me about Alisha, a terribly abused girl who needed a rescuer. Keith didn't know what to do for her. I told him that Jesus was a rescuer who can't make us accept Him. But because He offers, we have a possibility of hope.

    I didn't know if I was helping Keith or not. I think the most difficult issue for me was that his struggles were honest. And they were not exclusive to him. The difference was that Keith was being honest, whereas most of us tend to put up walls that are constructed with a carefully picked and practiced vocabulary. It's all part of that little environment that isn't affected by the outside world. *(Setting: Brian exits and Jeremy replaces him as Keith speaks)*

[Suggested Visuals: Face of a young man—perhaps expressionless as if he may be trying to live his life behind a perpetual mask.]

Keith: And then there's Jeremy—a young man who works part-time in our building. He's only twenty—more like a kid really. His mother died recently, and when I told him I was sorry, he said . . .

Jeremy: *(Facing the audience)* Thanks. I appreciate that.

Keith: We always say we're sorry. It seems empty most of the time—you know, just filler—so I asked him how he was—how he really was.

Jeremy: You don't want to know.

Keith: I told him I did.

Jeremy: Maybe I should say something that sounds strong. Or maybe something that has just the right combination of toughness and tenderness. *(Long pause)* The truth is, I feel like there's this barely controlled part of me that could erupt at any time. It's a seething mass of bitterness that feels like it's eating away at me like . . .

Keith: Cancer?

Jeremy: That's what killed my mother.

Keith: I wanted him to tell me.

Jeremy: I don't understand how it happened. *(Pause)* I mean, I know that cancer kills people—but why her? *(Angrily)* Who picked her? Was that God's choice? Because if it was, then I think God makes cruel choices.

Keith: As he unraveled his tapestry of sorrow, it knotted into anger.

[Suggested Visuals: A mother and son chatting casually.]

Jeremy: She was one of those women who are always kind to everyone. I know that sounds real cliché, but it's true. She never said a harsh word to anyone. She was always doing things for people—always wanting to help people. So here's this great lady—never did anything to anyone. And here's me, just getting to the end of my teenage years—just realizing how wonderful my mother really is—looking ahead to a relationship as adults, not as mother and child. And she gets sick.

Keith: Lots of people die too soon. But for Jeremy it wasn't merely his mother's death.

[Suggested Visuals: ICU room in a hospital, preferably with an empty bed.]

Jeremy: Have you ever watched someone die from cancer? On a day-to-day basis? See this slow, degenerating process that devours body, mind, and spirit? I knew Mom was going to die—I knew that early on. It was serious and she wasn't responding well to the radiation—and she went through it all. God knows what it was like for her. And still He let her suffer. There were nights when she would literally scream in agony—others where she was in some drug-induced trance. But even that wasn't the worst. It was the helplessness. *(Pause)*

One night I was sitting on the bed with her. I was just holding her—trying to comfort her. She was unable to speak but when she looked at me, it was as if she was screaming. She was pleading with me to stop the pain. *(Long pause)* It was all I could do not to give her at least one more injection. One more dose of morphine and no more pain—not ever. But I couldn't do it. *(Long pause)* There were three more months like that before she died on Christmas Eve. I remember even seeing gifts with her name on them.

[Suggested Visuals: Christmas present with "Mother" (or "Mom") on the tag.]

Keith: I can't imagine what that would be like.

Jeremy: The next day—Christmas morning—my father handed me a card. It was from Mom. It said she hoped I would always remember her.

Keith: I wanted Jeremy to know that God understands.

Jeremy: What does that mean? Who cares if God understands? What good is it if there's no action to back it up? If I see a little kid toddling toward a busy street, and I know without a doubt that he's going to get hit, but I do nothing to stop it, then I'm a monster. So why does God get away with it? Why is it He sees all these horrible things—all this injustice—and yet He gets to ignore it? *(Jeremy exits and is replaced by Brian)*

Keith: I knew there had to be something I could say to Jeremy—I just didn't know what it was. I had to admit that at times it does seem like God ignores suffering.

Brian: Keith needed to realize that God doesn't ignore any suffering.

Keith: I don't want to believe that God ignores suffering—but how can we know that?

[Suggested Visuals: Crucifixion scene—obvious torment and agony.]

Brian: Jesus experienced suffering.

Keith: Is that what I should tell Jeremy?

Brian: It's a start. We tell people that God understands—that God knows exactly what we're going through. But just saying that can become some sort of a mantra that loses its meaning if we're not careful.

Keith: How do I explain it? How do I make sure I never forget?

Brian: We must remember that when Jesus suffered, it wasn't just a physical agony. It was also from consuming all our sin—He did that for every person who accepts His sacrificial gift. And during that sin, God turned His back on Jesus—allowed Him to fall into the very pits of hell.

Keith: Agony . . .

Brian: Suffering . . .

Keith: Death . . .

Brian: Not just understood . . .

Keith: But experienced . . .

Brian: That's Emmanuel. God with us—Jesus Christ, who not only walked among us, but who also endured an agonizing death. Who not only endured an agonizing death, but who was separated from God.

Keith: And that's our hope?

Brian: Yes. It's hope because God knows suffering.

Keith: And He won't leave us.

Brian: He wants us to be with Him—with Jesus Christ—the infant born to suffer.

Keith: And so our hope is not that we will avoid death. It's that we overcome death.

Brian: We overcome with Jesus Christ.

Keith: There's one other . . . *(Lights fade to black)*

Song(s)

Part Four:

"For Eternity"

Setting: Brian is standing, facing the audience. Keith is sitting in a chair on the opposite side of the stage.

Song(s)

Brian: *(Omit all the way to Keith's first dialogue on next page if presented within one service)* My friend, Keith, asked me to come to his house to talk to him. Actually it was just to listen to him. He had been slipping away from God over the last several years, and in this one afternoon I began to get a better glimpse of how that had happened.

He told me about himself, how he was feeling vulnerable and scared in the world. I told him Jesus was born into our world as a vulnerable infant. Because Jesus knows vulnerability, we have hope. Keith also told me about Alisha, a terribly abused girl who needed a rescuer. Keith didn't know what to do for her. I told him that Jesus was a rescuer who can't make us accept Him. But because He offers, we have a possibility of hope.

After Alisha, Keith told me about Jeremy, a young man whose mother recently died. Jeremy was angry with God, not so much for letting her die, but for letting her suffer. I told Keith that God understood suffering. Jesus suffered immensely, not just a physical death, but also a spiritual one. He agonized with the weight of the world's sin—with having God turn His back on His Son. It is precisely because Jesus suffered that we can know He understands suffering. It is our hope not that He remove our suffering, but rather that He will not remove Himself from us while we are suffering.

Keith: I've been thinking a lot about Christine lately.

Brian: Christine is Keith's sister. I met her once a few years ago. She's amazingly intelligent. Has her Ph.D. in Anthropology I think—teaches at a liberal arts college. She's been published in numerous research journals, she's written several books, and is highly respected in her field.

Keith: *(Brian exits and Christine replaces him during Keith's line)* She's so well educated, I've never known how to talk to her. It's not that I consider myself lacking in intellectual abilities, it's just that she has such different experiences, has studied such a wide variety of philosophers, scientists, and ethicists, I don't think I can compete. For example, even though I've been distant from God lately, I've never doubted that He exists. We can't even agree on that.

Christine: I just don't understand your fascination with superstitious mythology.

Keith: She thinks we're all here because of chance.

[Suggested Visuals: Shot of a single candle (or many candles) on a table, preferably with a New Age look to represent an atheist's disdainful impression of an altar.]

Christine: You can't live your life based on some absurd idea that some nebulous deity has designed everything around us. If that were the case, we'd be nothing more than puppets. I am who I am because of what I've done—not because of some supreme being. Look at me, Keith. Do I look like I need to spend my time searching for significance at some candle-lit altar?

Keith: Once again she's misunderstood my point. I want her to know that there is something more to this life than what she has.

Christine: What more could I want? I have a challenging career, a top salary in my field, a great home, a good husband and three children, and my book royalties will make retirement very comfortable.

Keith: Underneath all of that I still think she's searching for something.

Christine: Please, Keith, don't start with the God thing again. You're not exactly a paragon of morality. Don't forget, I'm your sister. I know what you're really like.

Keith: I tried to tell Christine that there is still more—that she really is missing something far greater.

[Suggested Visuals: Baroque or Renaissance painting of worshipers in supplication, or primitive humans (e.g., cavemen) worshiping an idol.]

Christine: I'll tell you what, Keith, I'll go so far as to say I understand why you need to believe in a god. That's something that every major culture throughout the history of the world has needed. I don't fault you for that. But you really need to understand that it's a total fabrication—a way of teaching societal values. One of the most respected biologists of the twentieth century, Stephen Jay Gould, said that humans arose as an outcome of thousands of linked events, any one of which could have occurred differently and sent history on an alternative pathway that would not have led to consciousness.

Keith: She just doesn't understand that there is a direction for her life—a standard that helps us day by day.

[Suggested Visuals: Newspaper headlines of scandals in the Church.]

Christine: Why would I want to follow a set of rules set by a bunch of people who are telling me what's moral or what isn't? Have you read the news lately, Keith? If those priests and what they did to those boys is representative of your god, then I don't want to hear another word. That's just one more example of what I've known all along. Bertrand Russell, the highly respected philosopher, once said that people who have held to Christianity have been for the most part extremely wicked. Throughout history every kind of cruelty was practiced upon all sorts of people in the name of religion. Look at the facts, Keith. The organized churches of the world have consistently opposed human progress from criminal law to race relations. Christianity, as an organized religion, has been, and still is, the principal enemy of moral progress in the world.

Keith: I told her that in some ways she's right. Organized religion has often been detrimental. But I'm talking about a relationship with God.

[Suggested Visuals: Picture of a vast expanse of mist-covered water.]

Christine: If there is a god, and I have seen no evidence to suggest there is, but if there is, then he is only a god who created an earth. He does not interact with it. And what's more, there is no such thing as pure good and there is no such thing as pure evil. There is only energy—and we choose to either embrace positive energy or negative energy.

Keith: *(Christine exits and Brian replaces her during Keith's line)* I don't know how to respond to her. She throws out all that philosophical stuff, quotes authors like she's reading a grocery list, and I don't have any common ground.

[Suggested Visuals: Compass and/or map (there should be a nautical look about it).]

Brian: I thought Keith was on the right track when he said Christine was searching for something. In reality, all of us are searching. We search for belonging— belonging to God, and belonging with God. He made us that way. We cannot be truly fulfilled without a relationship with Him. The problem is, we really know how to fool ourselves.

Keith: How do I help her realize that she is searching?

Brian: I think Keith might be able to help his sister by finding out where she gets her worth.

Keith: What do you mean by "her worth"?

Brian: It's a question we all have to ask ourselves. What is the source of our worth?

Keith: Christine gets hers from her accomplishments.

Brian: Then she'll always be working.

Keith: And from her colleagues' approvals.

Brian: Then she'll always be wanting.

Keith: And from her assets.

Brian: Then she'll always be needy.

Keith: So she needs to belong—and it needs to be permanent.

Brian: It's not that there's anything wrong with a good career, a nice home, or a lucrative salary. It's just that they can't guarantee anything long-lasting. *(Pause, then with emphasis)* There is an enormous difference between belongings and belonging.

Keith: But with Christ, there is true belonging.

Brian: And that is our hope. Through His death and resurrection, Jesus restored our relationship with God.

Keith: So that we can belong.

Brian: With Him.

Keith: For eternity. (*Keith exits*)

[Suggested Visuals: A quick series of pictures that shows an advent wreath, a baby in a manger, Jesus reaching out to a person, Jesus on the cross, and finally an empty cross.]

Brian: (*Long pause*) I had gone to Keith's wondering what Advent really meant in the practical, everyday world. When I left Keith, I still hadn't answered all his questions. But I had answered mine. Advent is the coming Christ—and it means as much today as it did when Jesus was born. He is the helpless baby, the Savior alone in the world, willing to be vulnerable. He is the rescuer, the Savior alone in a world of people who did not understand Him, yet He reaches out His hand to offer a gift we cannot comprehend. He is Emmanuel, God with us—the Savior alone on the cross who sacrificed Himself so we will have life. He is the restorer, the Savior alone in the depths of hell, so we can overcome death. That is Advent—knowing we can rely on the Savior alone for direction in our lives.

That's really all I gave Keith—direction. When our compass is on the right setting, we get to our destination eventually. That doesn't mean there won't be storms or that we won't get off course. That's why I don't like pat answers. If we say Jesus is the answer, then how do we explain all the struggles we face? It makes us feel like we're not worthy to even talk to God if we ever succumb to a temptation or if a terrible tragedy occurs or if we have questions that shake our faith.

[Suggested Visuals: This final picture should be very scenic—preferably a long winding country lane that disappears out of sight to represent that we cannot see where our life's journey will take us, We can choose to walk it alone or with Christ.]

Brian: Jesus is the direction for our lives—and through Him we can find our answers. That's what Keith is going to have to do. It's what I do every time I meet someone with a serious issue. With God's help, we try to do our best and work out the "hows"—and every circumstance is different. Every person is unique—but we do it one soul at a time.

Song(s)

Christmas Then & Now

by Kathy Ide (with David B. Carl)

Characters: -Mary, Jesus' mother-to-be
-Joseph, Mary's betrothed
-Norm, Modern-day husband and father
-June, Norm's wife

Purpose: While Mary and Joseph (on Stage Right) struggle together as they await Jesus' birth, Norm and June (on Stage Left) struggle with the family stresses of their modern-day celebration of this same event.

Production: Stage Right: Mary, very pregnant and dressed in dirty, tattered robes, sits on a rough wooden stool. Joseph, also dirty and unkempt, sits on the ground next to her. Both look completely exhausted. A "stable" background is a nice touch, but optional. A skin of water and an earthen cup are on the ground, just out of Mary's reach.

Stage Left: Norm and June sit in side-by-side chairs representing an automobile. Both are dressed in holiday celebration clothes, but Norm looks a bit disheveled. A steering wheel on a stand in front of Norm is helpful (one with a horn can be quite amusing), but steering can be mimed.

When action takes place on Stage Right, Norm and June freeze. When action is on Stage Left, Mary and Joseph freeze. If stage lights (and an attentive stage crew) are available, lighting can switch back and forth as scenes shift.

Props: Padding for Mary's stomach, wooden stool, skin of water, earthen cup, two chairs, steering wheel on stand (optional, but really helpful), and baby Jesus

Length: 15 minutes

Stage Left

Norm: *(Irritated by the holiday traffic)* They've probably started without us. I can't believe this traffic. It's Christmas Eve! Why aren't all these people home with their families?

June: *(irritated by Norm)* I hope they *have* started without us. Why should their dinner be ruined just because we're late? *(Turns slightly toward the back seat)* You kids are being careful with that Jell-O salad, aren't you? *(Turns back to Norm)* Norman, your son is drawing designs on the foil over my Jell-O salad.

Norm: *(Without looking back)* Billy, get away from that salad this instant or I'll make you wish you'd never heard of Jell-O.

June: You really shouldn't talk to the children that way, dear.

Norm: *(Sighs, then in mock sweetness)* Snuggle Bunny, if it's all right with you, would you mind not playing too much with the aluminum foil on your mother's Jell-O salad? *(June slaps him on the arm)* Ow!

Stage Right

Mary: *(Reaches for the water bag, but stops short in pain)* Ooh!

Joseph: *(Very concerned)* Mary, are you all right?

Mary: Oh, yes. I just moved wrong. *(She reaches again, but another pain hits)* Oh!

Joseph: Here, let me get that for you. *(He gets the water bag and pours her a drink. She takes it.)*

Mary: Thank you, Joseph. *(She sips)* Do you expect Bethlehem to be very crowded?

Joseph: More than I wish it would be.

Mary: Do you think we'll have any trouble getting a room?

Joseph: I've been wondering about that all day. There probably won't be anything decent left by the time we get there.

Mary: *(Sensing his worry)* Joseph, what will we do?

Joseph: *(Realizing he has worried her)* Oh, I'm sorry, Mary. I didn't mean to upset you. Don't worry. God will provide something.

Mary: I'm sure you're right.

Joseph: I bet we'll look all over town for a room, and then someone wealthy will take pity on us and invite us in. I can't see God allowing His Son to be born in a public inn.

Mary: *(Chuckles a bit, relieved by his explanation)* Tell me about Jerusalem, Joseph.

Joseph: *(Laughing)* Mary, I've already told you everything I know. I started making things up two days ago.

Mary: *(In a pretense of shock)* I can't believe you'd lie to a pregnant woman!

Joseph: *(Laughing with her)* I love you, Mary. *(Joseph and Mary gaze lovingly at each other for a brief moment, then Joseph stands and prays aloud. Mary freezes.)* Oh Lord, my God. You've blessed me above all other men. *(Looks fondly at Mary, who is still frozen)* I've married the love of my life, and soon we will begin to raise Your only Son. Sometimes, Lord, I'm petrified with fear. Who am I to raise the Son of God? What happens when I make mistakes? How do I treat Him? What will He be like? *(Pause)* Mary, are you scared?

Mary: *(Reanimating)* Well . . . *(She tries to stand. JOSEPH helps her up as she speaks.)* I've never been to a big city before . . . I'm nine months pregnant . . . I've ridden a donkey for five days . . . and I am going to give birth soon to the Son of God. *(Slight chuckle)* I'm a little tense. What about you?

Joseph: *(Trying to sound more confident than he feels)* Oh, I know God will take care of us. There's really nothing to be afraid of.

Stage Left

Norm: I'm scared, June.

June: *(Looks out the window, not paying attention)* Oh? About what?

Norm: *(Shocked at her indifference)* Hey, I'm trying to communicate with you!

June: I'm sorry, Norman. I'm listening.

Norm: *(Pause)* I think my hairline is receding.

June: Maybe it's just that your forehead is growing.

Norm: Oh, great. Mock me. *(To the "kids")* What are you laughing at back there?

June: I'm sorry. I just thought it was going to be . . . something else. *(She looks out the window again)*

Norm: June, life is getting to me. It's too complex. And it gets worse at Christmas. If we go to everyone's house, we never have a moment to ourselves. But if we stay home, the whole family gets angry and it takes till Thanksgiving the next year to appease everyone. Then it just starts all over again. *(Pause)* What do you think we should do?

June: I think we should stop at a restaurant and feed the kids.

Norm: You didn't hear a word I said. *(To the kids)* You be quiet and play with the aluminum foil!

Stage Right

Mary: *(Frightened)* I can't go in there.

Joseph: I'm sorry, Mary. I didn't think it would turn out like this.

Mary: There are animals in there, Joseph. It's filthy! And it smells. Look at all the bugs and flies. *(She screams and doubles over in pain)* Quick, Joseph! Get me inside! *(Joseph helps Mary walk and then lie down)*

Joseph: Just lie down here for a while.

Mary: I don't mean to be a whiner, Joseph, but your wealthy someone can come get us any time now.

Joseph: I'm so sorry, Mary. I thought God would want what I want. I'm such a fool.

Mary: Joseph, I'm scared. I've never had a baby before.

Joseph: I know. Um . . . *(Nervous)* . . . tell me what I can do.

Mary: Just build a fire to warm this place up, and find somewhere to lay Jesus when He comes.

Joseph: Great! I can do that. I'll go get some firewood. *(He exits hastily)*

Mary: Oh, Father God, please be with me now. I know Your Son will be born, and that He'll grow. But I'm still scared. *(Pause)* Joseph! JOSEPH

Joseph:	*(Entering frantically)* What's the matter?
Mary:	I just thought of something. We know that the baby will be fine, but . . . but what if I die in childbirth? Are there any prophecies about that? Oh, Joseph, I'm so frightened. I've never felt pain like this before.
Joseph:	*(Trying to be calm and to calm Mary)* We have no choice but to trust in God. Please, Mary, be brave and pray.
Mary:	*(Suddenly stern)* Joseph, I think you should leave now.
Joseph:	Oh, Mary, I'm sorry. All I meant was—
Mary:	Joseph . . . it's time.
Joseph:	Time?
Mary:	For the baby.
Joseph:	Oh! Okay. I guess I should leave. *(Starts to exit, then turns)* Are you sure you'll be all right? I mean, can you do this by yourself?
Mary:	Don't worry, Joseph. I've seen babies born many times. I know what to do.
Joseph:	I love you, Mary. *(She winces in pain)* I'll be right outside if you need me. *(He exits hastily)*
Mary:	Oh, God, I feel so alone. I wish I were home with my mother to help me. Instead I'm in a strange town full of strange people, giving birth to the Son of God in a manure-filled stable! *(On the verge of tears)* I don't understand any of this. *(Pause)* Poor Joseph. I can't believe he has put up with all this. He's the most noble man I've ever known, and yet . . . *(Smiles)* sometimes he's such a little boy. Joseph!
Joseph:	*(Entering quickly)* Yes, Mary?
Mary:	*(pause)* I love you.
Joseph:	I love you too.
Mary:	*(Winces in pain)* Joseph, you'd better leave.
Joseph:	Are you sure? *(Mary screams)*
Joseph:	I'm going! *(Exits)*

Mary: Please, Lord, let me live to hold Your Son in my arms. I want to see Him play and run. I want to teach Him to talk, and I want to kiss His little hands. I feel like I'm just a girl myself, but I want so much to be a mother.

Stage Left

June: I can't go in there. Look at this place. I will *not* eat in a place called "Joe's." What a dump! Merry Christmas, kids. Can you say "botulism"?

Norm: Hey, be grateful. This is the only joint open between here and Modesto. It is Christmas Eve, you know.

June: This place isn't a diner. It's a petri dish with a jukebox.

Norm: All right. Everybody shut the doors. We're leaving. *(To June)* I thought you wanted to feed the kids.

June: Hey, back there, the Jell-O salad is fair game. *(Pause, as if listening to the kids)* You do too! You've always liked my Jell-O salad. *(To herself)* I can't believe them. They'll turn on you in a heartbeat.

Norm: *(In response to the kids)* I don't know how much longer, and I'd better not hear that question again.

June: *(After an uneasy silence)* Norman, why don't we . . .

Norm: Sell our kids to the next passerby?

June: No, no. Why don't we tell the kids the Christmas story.

Norm: What? Where Santa came from?

June: No, the other one . . . from the Bible.

Norm: *(Shrugs)* Okay with me.

June: All right. *(To the kids)* But you'll have to be quiet and listen. Mary and Joseph traveled a long distance while Mary was pregnant. *(Pause)* No, honey, they didn't have stagecoaches back then. This was before that. Norm, how did they travel?

Norm: I think they were carried on those big stretcher things.

June: No, they were poor. I think they rode in a chariot or something.

Norm: *(Picking up the story)* And when they got to the town, there was some kind of convention going on, and all the hotels were full. Joseph went from door to door, and nobody had any rooms for them.

June: So one innkeeper felt sorry for them and told them they could stay in this darling little stable. *(Smiling, really getting into the story)* They had lots of clean, golden hay to sleep on. There was a gentle cow and the cutest little lamb in the stable with them. And for just that night, the animals could talk.

Norm: June, you've watched too many cartoons. The animals did not talk.

June: *(Glares at Norm, then continues undaunted)* Anyway . . . Mary was sweet, and she had a glow around her face.

Norm: Where does it say that?

June: Look at any manger scene in the world and you can see for yourself.

Norm: *(Sighs)* So about that time, it started to snow. And this little drummer boy came into the stable.

June: Norman, it has not snowed in Bethlehem since the Ice Age.

Norm: Then why would the little drummer boy go into the stable, huh?

June: Where did you get a little drummer boy, anyway, Mr. Never-Watches-Cartoons?

Norm: I can't believe you said that. What would Christmas be without a drummer boy?

June: Quieter?

Norm: So then, one day, the Grinch who stole Christmas married your mother, and they all lived happily ever after.

June: All right, that's enough. *(Pause)* Hey, what's that? *(Pointing)*

Norm: I . . . I think it's a Bun Boy Restaurant.

June: We're saved!

Norm: Double chili cheeseburgers, here we come! This is gonna be a good Christmas after all. Come on, kids. Let's sing. *(Sings)* Jingle bells, Batman smells, Robin laid an egg . . .

Stage Right:

Mary is sleeping peacefully, her padding gone or her back to the audience. Baby Jesus lies nearby.

Joseph: *(Entering)* Mary? *(Seeing her)* Are you asleep? Of course you are. *(sits beside her)* It's been an incredible night, hasn't it? *(Pause)* Mary . . . I have a confession to make. *(Pause)* I'm scared. Watching the woman you love give birth is pretty frightening any time. But this . . . *(Looking at Jesus)* I suppose all parents think their babies are perfect. But this child . . . is perfection itself. *(Back to Mary)* Oh, Mary, this is all too much. I know God chose you to be the mother of His child. As amazing as that is, I can see why. You're so good and kind and godly. That's why I love you. But I didn't realize, until just this moment, that God chose me too. The Lord Shaddai wants me to raise His only Son, to be the earthly father of the long-awaited Messiah! Why? Why me? I have nothing to offer. I'm just a carpenter. All my big plans to teach my child the carpentry business! What does the Son of God need with that? *(Picks up baby Jesus and holds him with new-father awkwardness)* Fathers are supposed to teach their children everything they need to know. But what can *I* teach *You*? You've already shown me more than I'll ever be able to show You. You've taught me about . . . miracles. God's infinite power. His overwhelming love for mankind. What can I offer You in return? Absolutely nothing. Nothing but love. *(He shrugs. Pause. His tone and facial expression turn from self-mocking to realization.)* But . . . if that's what You need from me . . . love . . . oh, Jesus, I can give You that in abundance! *(Holds baby Jesus closer to him)* My sweet little baby. I can hold You when You cry. I can provide food and shelter. We don't live like King Herod, but it's better than this smelly stable! *(Reaches out and touches Mary's sleeping form)* I don't know what kind of father I'll be, Jesus. But I do promise You . . . and our heavenly Father . . . and all the angels watching us right now . . . that with God's help, I will love You, and Your mother, with all my heart, all my strength, and all my soul, every day of my life. *(Looks at Jesus and chuckles softly)* So You're going to fall asleep on me, too, are You? That's all right. What are fathers for, if not to protect their families so they can sleep in heavenly peace?

Make the *most wonderful time of the year even better!*

His First Noel
Joshua L. McKinney
$5.99 each or $4.99 each when ordered
in quantities of 13 or more
ISBN 0892655887

"His First Noel" tells the story of Jim, a middle-aged man who is ill, coming to the end of his life, and resisting God. As his family gathers for Christmas they continue a family tradition of taking in a homeless person for the holidays. What none of them realize is that they are entertaining angels. This heartwarming story presents the gospel and prompts people to analyze their own spiritual condition.

Heaven Came Down
Jack Dale
$5.99 each or $4.99 each when ordered
in quantities of 35 or more
ISBN 0892655879

This full-length drama is set in the Biblical era and begins 15 months prior to the birth of Christ. "Heaven Came Down" portrays events that may have taken place in heaven and what did transpire on earth before Christ's birth and uses traditional hymns to help tell the story.